EVE MARX

Flirtspeak

THE SEXY LANGUAGE
OF FLIRTING

MJF BOOKS
NEW YORK

Published by MJF Books
Fine Communications
322 Eighth Avenue
New York, NY 10001

Flirtspeak
LC Control Number 2007939429
ISBN-13: 978-1-56731-896-8
ISBN-10: 1-56731-896-7

QM   10 9 8 7 6 5 4 3 2 1

For Trifle

CONTENTS

INTRODUCTION

Everybody knows about great opening lines. "Have we met?" "Do you come here often?" and "What's your sign?" are words—lines actually—that men use all the time. Corny and clichéd as these lines may be, they work. And why? Because they grab a woman's attention, invite her to look at a guy, and most important of all, open the door to more words, more looks, and just possibly (!) further communication.

Imagine this: It's Thursday morning, 8:37 A.M., and you're standing in line at the coffee/tea bar where you get your morning cup. The clock is ticking and there's less than fifteen minutes left to negotiate ordering your low-fat decaf latté skim mocha and get over to work. On top of everything else, you just noticed a snag in your pantyhose that you know will annoy you all day. But even in your state of mild distraction, you did not fail to notice the adorable guy standing in line behind you. He looks even less awake than you feel, but now that you've had a few moments to observe him more carefully (surreptiously of course), you see he's got a teensy bit of shaving cream right in front of his left ear. Should you say something to him—or not?

You don't know this guy from Adam. But maybe you want to. Or maybe talking to him is just something you could do to pass the time in line. Should you break the news to him that he's got something on his face to wipe off? Or will you just let it go, turn back to your Blackberry, and never have the chance to find out if he's worth getting to know better, if he's someone you would consider dating or even marrying. Who knows? By not speaking to him, you may be missing out on meeting the future father of your children!

The bottom line is that, if you don't take advantage of the many opportunities that are right in front of you, you're missing out on a ton of chances to have a little fun.

The first time you speak to a guy, you leave an indelible impression. If he's like most guys, he will remember the first time he meets his wife, his girlfriends, and the other women he has long-term relationships with. He might even remember great mysterious women he shared a couple of phrases with, who disappeared into the crowd and for whom he carried a torch for years, if not forever.

Your first words to a man are like a message in a bottle. It almost doesn't matter what you say as long as you say . . . something! The point is to get across to that guy that you're awake, aware, and interested. (The fact that you're smart and sexy should soon follow.) Your actual words and the way you deliver them should captivate, fascinate, and intrigue a man. Your words can be cute and funny, or they can ask a question or point out something totally obvious but in a clever, feminine way. You want to give that guy something he can respond to, or mull over, a comment he'll have to sit up and pay attention to . . . or lose out to another guy who digs better what you have to say.

Besides improving your odds of making a love connection, there are tons of other reasons to have a full repertoire of verbal badinage and gambits—flirtspeak—ready at your lips. For example, you could make a new friend, or find your way to a better job, or start getting to know the guy who would be perfect for your sister. *Flirtspeak* will help you amp up your verbal arsenal with tons of icebreakers, conversation tactics, and sexy skills so you always know what to say to a man—in any situation! As you will see, the benefits to having superior (and sexy) conversation skills are myriad.

Now let the fun begin!

Part One

Breaking the Ice

Chapter One

What's Your Flirtstyle?

What Kind of Verbal Flirt Are You?

The following is a little quiz designed to help you figure out your natural verbal flirting style. There are no right or wrong answers here—the idea is to assist you in honing in on your natural talents, defining and assessing your assets, and guiding you toward realizing your ultimate flirting potential. Hopefully, your answers will help you focus your efforts on guys who are most naturally drawn to you. Why waste your valuable time on bad fits?

WHAT'S YOUR NATURAL FLIRTING STYLE?

1. **Your favorite movie that features lots of hot and heavy flirting is:**
   a. *Breakfast at Tiffany's*
   b. *Pretty Woman*
   c. *Desk Set*
   d. *Notting Hill*
   e. *The Prince of Tides*
   f. *Love, Actually*

2. If you were to go out and buy a new perfume it would be:
   a. Paris by Paris Hilton
   b. Miami Glo by J. Lo
   c. Reaction by Kenneth Cole
   d. Baby Girl by Clean
   e. Coco Mademoiselle by Chanel
   f. Roberto Cavalli by Roberto Cavalli

3. On a first date, you'd be most comfortable wearing:
   a. *Something leather*
   b. *Something formfitting*
   c. *Anything with cleavage*
   d. *Something buttoned up*
   e. *Something bedizened with chiffon or velvet*
   f. *Sexy jeans*

4. The first words out of your mouth to a new guy are something like:
   a. "Here's my phone number—don't lose it."
   b. "Did we meet before? You look familiar."
   c. "How do you feel about love at first sight?"
   d. You'd never make the first comment
   e. "How can I help you?"
   f. "Hey, you're cute, but you just stepped on my foot."

5. If you could have any pet, it would be:
   a. A purse pup
   b. A stuffed animal

c. A guard dog
d. A kitten
e. A fish
f. A ferret

6. **A possible line you might throw out to a guy might be one of these:**
   a. "You're not living with anyone, are you?"
   b. "Are you really from Italy?"
   c. "I heard you were getting married."
   d. "My mother told me to never talk to guys like you."
   e. "We haven't been introduced. Should we?"
   f. "Got milk?"

7. **Your last boyfriend accused you of being:**
   a. High maintenance
   b. Fickle
   c. Pushy
   d. A tad comatose
   e. Needy
   f. Not serious enough

8. **You're most likely to talk to a guy you don't know:**
   a. At a club
   b. On an airplane but only if you're petrified
   c. At the library
   d. Because your mother forced you to
   e. In an elevator
   f. Online

8. If you could be a celebrity, the woman you'd most like to be is:

a. Heidi Klum
b. Britney Spears
c. Julia Roberts
d. Natalie Portman
e. Scarlett Johansson
f. Kathy Griffin

Figured out yet who you are? Are you shy and unassuming or are you more the jokey type? Are you a smooth talker, a kibitzer, someone who loves being helpful, or a bit of a ditz? Five women who were given this quiz said they thought they were a bit of everything, although not at the same time.

Even if you think you're more shy, than, say, helpful, absolutely don't limit or compartmentalize yourself. Just as you change your hairstyle and play with your heel height, depending on your mood, and where you are and who you are with, you can and should adjust or fine-tune your persona to suit different needs.

Here's a breakdown on what kind of flirty girl you might be. Remember these definitions definitely aren't set in stone. Think of them as guidelines to develop your own signature flirtspeak style.

Mostly a's:	The Smooth Talker
Mostly b's:	The Ditz
Mostly c's:	The Interrogator
Mostly d's:	The Shy Girl
Mostly e's:	The Helper
Mostly f's:	The Comedienne

The Smooth Talker

Smooth Talkers come in a variety of shapes and sizes. They're the chameleons among flirtatious women because they can shift and change tactics depending on what type of guy they're talking to. Smooth Talkers are skillful conversationalists—they are adventurous and inventive with their social interactions. The original "say anything girls," these ladies truly deserve their exciting if slippery reputations. They have a flair for small talk and wrapping a string of phrases together that can leave the listener feeling a bit dazed and confused. It's a "shock and awe" thing.

Smooth Talkers are, in a word, slick. Experts at the riff and the pun, they are also marvelous storytellers who can be extremely entertaining. Not everything a Smooth Talker says should be reckoned as the truth. Smooth Talkers somehow aren't held to the same standards as other flirts. They get a lot more leeway! It isn't an exaggeration to say that Smooth Talkers operate in a realm of their own because they're just so smooth that they are expected to get away with saying the most outrageous things and have everybody listening hanging on their every word.

If you're a Smooth Talker, then you have probably been honing your skills for quite some time. If you wish you were more of a Smooth Talker, there's good news—Smooth Talkers are made, not born. Smooth Talking requires practice. Ladies who would like to develop their Smooth Talking muscles need to work at it with the same dedication they put into their thighs at the gym. Beginning Smooth Talkers can hone their skills by studying back to back episodes of *Sex in the City* (most people think of Samantha as the original Smooth Talker, but Carrie is the queen) or really old episodes of *Moonlighting* starring Cybill Shepherd and Bruce Willis. The repartee between those two is priceless! Jennifer Aniston played the role of the Smoothest (female) Talker on *Friends*. (Joey, of course, was the guy.) Joyce Carol Oates wrote a short story called "Smooth Talker," which was made into a movie starring Laura Dern.

Smooth Talking is fun. It's playful, sly, glib, facetious, and attractive all at the same time. Certain professions encourage Smooth Talkiness. If you are a personal injury lawyer, personal trainer, guru, sales person, or real estate agent, you've probably racked up a lot of time practicing smooth talking. Smooth Talkers do well on TV, make great radio deejays, can sell ice to Eskimos. The best ones are terrifically entertaining since talking smooth can be quite funny.

The trouble with being too good a Smooth Talker is that guys don't take you seriously. They know you're flirting and figure every word out of your mouth is a line, definitely enjoyable but lacking in sincerity. When a Smooth Talking girl really falls for Mr. Right, she may have to work overtime convincing him that he's more than a plaything. Guys today are so sensitive! They just hate being thought of as anybody's toy!

Top Tips for Smooth Talking Girls

* **Smooth Talk with confidence.** Even if what you say only bears a passing resemblance to the truth, relate your information convincingly and everybody will believe you.

* **Don't go batty.** Refrain from batting your eyes if you're a Smooth Talker—that's really over the top!

* **Borrow material from other sources.** The Smooth Talkers have stock lines for every potential flirtation situation.

* **Channel your inner politician.** Speak more for effect than meaning—and charm your audience.

* **The Quotability Quotient.** Do remember that everything you say will be repeated. People always quote Smooth Talkers!

* **Keep your game face on.** Don't laugh out loud at your own outrageousness. Duck into the ladies' room when your own bullshit becomes even too much for you to handle.

* **Keep it flowing.** Keep the conversational current flowing at a fairly rapid rate so the guy you're flirting with doesn't have a chance to ponder very long on anything you said. Most Smooth Talking is crème de la crème gibberish but, if you spout your words fast enough, he won't even notice.

Guys respond naturally to Smooth Talkers at first because Smooth Talkers use tactics similar to men's! As the old expression goes, "It takes one to know one"—many guys admire women who sound, er, like men. Smooth Talkers quite often are exceptionally beautiful and feminine, which further enhances their appeal and allows them to work their magic. The best Smooth Talkers may invest a lot of time watching themselves in the mirror, coordinating their eyes, lips, and other facial expressions with the lines that spill out of their mouths.

A Smooth Talking girl can flirt her way into the heart (or groin) of a guy she met only an hour before and get him to buy her dinner. The ability to Smooth Talk can really pay off big time. Keep in mind that many a Smooth Talking girl has become the wife of a

CEO or other hotshot. The men who ask for these ladies' hands in marriage know exactly how much their special talent is worth.

For as many guys out there who love the charm of a Smooth Talking woman, there are some who are naturally suspicious of a woman whose talk is even slicker than their own. So if you're a Smooth Talker and you find that your sibilant syllables turn your flirt quarry off more than turn him on, either drop the pose immediately or release that guy back into the pond.

The Smooth Talking girl is the mistress of the "little white lie," or falsification by omission. She likes to keep her back protected, her bases covered. It's hard to get to really know a Smooth Talker; except to their closest friends or lovers, they can come off as superficial and insincere. The Smooth Talker is most at ease when she controls the situation, which she does through her superior use of language. Out in the man/woman marketplace, this woman's outstanding verbal skills make her a formidable customer! The Smooth Talker is often quite guarded about her personal life. While she can talk rings around other people, she isn't easy to penetrate.

The Ditz

Everybody loves the appeal of the Ditz. Famous lovable Ditzes you will recognize straight off the bat have been Lisa Kudrow playing Phoebe on *Friends*, Sandra Bullock in *Speed*, and Meg Ryan in just about any movie she's ever been in. Marilyn Monroe, of course, played the ultimate Ditz. As you can see from the examples above, a lot of famous Ditzes are blondes—but that doesn't mean if you're a brunette or a redhead, you can't work it! Despite their ditzy ways, Ditzy girls have a certain naive charm that often gets them out of sticky situations—from missing appointments to losing their keys to clumsy physical encounters, either in the car or on the street. And at the same time Ditzy girls are incredibly sexy and that's without even trying! Men just love it when a girl adorably screws up—it makes them feel so in control and superior!

The great thing about the Ditz is that it's an easy flirting style for any girl to use. The Ditz personality is naturally enthusiastic, bubbly, even gregarious. Ditzy girls can appear drunk even when they're cold sober. They often come off as naive, or disingenuous, or easily confused. They tend to be artistic by nature and often pursue artistic professions, like photography, painting, or acting. Seldom are they whizzes at parallel parking or dealing with unfamiliar gas pumps. Although the Ditz might not always remember her ATM password or her keys, when it comes to flirting, she's a total pro. One of the great things the Ditz can really excel at is the knack of being at the right place at the wrong time. . . and then capitalizing on her mistake.

Top Tips for Ditzes

✧ *Embrace your Ditzy self.* If you were born a Ditz, don't fight Mother Nature. You are what you are, so don't try to be anybody else. Your natural ditziness is like an intoxicating aroma that can't fail to attract men. Use what you have to your advantage, and you can't go wrong.

✧ *Go Blond.* Unless you are a very dark brunette (like Sandra Bullock), color your locks blond. Blond, as everyone knows, is the natural hair color of Ditzes! However, if coloring your tresses is too drastic for you, check out these great tips for Ditzes of the nonblond variety:

- Wear cat's-eye-shaped glasses.
- Wear a lot of eye makeup.
- Say "Whoops!" a lot.
- Misplace things in public so you have to make a big production of finding your . . . glasses.
- Cultivate some physically funny habits, like twirling your fingers ostentatiously when you are bored or yawning.
- When a man is talking to you, open your eyes extra wide and then at the end of his statement of a joke's punchline . . . blink!

✧ *Don't tell jokes.* Ditzes should just not tell jokes, unless for planned effect. Ditzy girls are just incapable of telling a joke. They never get the punchline right or they leave out something essential. The only reason a Ditzy girl should tell a joke is because she knows in advance that she's going to muff it up and get a good laugh.

✧ *Cultivate a multitude of male friends.* Program them into your cell phone. You never know when they'll come in handy to get you out of jams!

✧ *Laugh at yourself.* After all, you are funny!

Guys fall for Ditzy girls because they are so charming and seemingly helpless (but we all know this isn't always the case!). Because Ditzy girls often appear to be damsels in distress, appearing weak makes the men around them feel strong. For this reason, men who are drawn to the Ditz subconsciously envision themselves as knights in shining armor arriving on horseback to the rescue.

Despite her many foibles, the Ditz is surprisingly self-confident, and while she knows how to use her Ditziness to its fullest flirt potential, that doesn't mean that she'll easily fall for a cheesy line or a less-than-stellar guy. She's a certified flirtation expert, and she chooses her flirt quarries carefully. So, despite her rather flaky first impression—never feel sorry for a Ditzy girl. Though, at first glance, she may appear to be helpless, she's quite capable of taking care of herself.

The universe has a way of looking out for Ditzy girls. No matter how lost and confused a Ditz truly is, somehow she always manages to come out on top! The pot of gold at the end of the rainbow for a really clever Ditzy girl is that she usually get the guy she wants—and he really wants to take care of her. As long as she remains true to her Ditzy self, he'll always feel like a hero in her presence.

The Interrogator

By definition, the Interrogator is nosy—she's a cross between a private detective, a prosecutor, and a concerned girlfriend/wife. She's not embarrassed to ask questions. She thinks no more of prying into a guy's life than she would about opening his closet or pulling a long hair off a total stranger's sweater. Boundaries—intellectual and physical—often mean nothing to her, and very few of her intimates would ever call her "shy." The great thing about the Interrogator is that she's utterly fearless. She says what's on her mind and, if she's got a question about something, she doesn't hesitate to ask.

Girls who ask a lot of questions often get a bad rap. Remember the old cliché "Curiosity killed the cat?" Well, the other side of that cliché is "Knowledge is power." Girls who never ask questions rarely find out anything useful.

Interrogators come in many shapes and sizes. She might be light and perky, like Jane Pauley, or more like Mariska Hargitay on *Law & Order* or Marg Helgenberger on *CSI*. Her mode of questioning can be straightforward and direct, or it can be low-key, casual, and thoroughly disarming. The Interrogator isn't afraid to quiz a guy she just met on where he lives, his age, if he's still living with his mother. She will definitely ask him what kind of car he drives.

The Interrogator also tends to notice important details other girls are slower to pick up on, like if the guy has a crate of kid's games stashed way in the back of his SUV, or that he has cat hair on his pants even though he just said he didn't own any pets. The Interrogator zooms in on a guy's accent, the condition of his shoes—anything she can to find out more about him.

As helpful as the Interrogator's tactics may be, she must tread very carefully. Asking a lot of questions can make a girl look suspicious. (Big hint: Most guys are put off by girls who don't appear to trust them. Some guys also just have a natural tendency to buck and rear at any questions directed at them from the mouth of a female.)

So if your natural tendency is to ask guys a lot of questions, make them good ones! By putting a positive spin on your interrogations, you're more likely to keep him interested—and you're bound to find something out! Be sure to start off by asking things a guy can answer easily—simple, , direct, nonchallenging questions such as "Where'd you get that fantastic tie?" or "Do you work out here often?" These questions are like doors a guy can open and walk through—toward you! Incredibly enough, the most simple and direct question of all is a real no-brainer—and also the one that many flirtatious women don't apply enough— "What's your name?" Don't hesitate to use it, even if you've just that moment been introduced. Chances are he didn't catch your name either, so there's no need to be embarrassed. After all, you're in the same boat.

Top Tips for Interrogators

* ✳ *Take it slow.* When you're talking to a guy, try to ask him one question at a time. Two questions at once is overwhelming. Three makes you seem like the police.

* ✳ *Keep it light.* Your question doesn't have to be serious. A jokey question can be a great icebreaker.

* ✳ *A little bit of eye contact goes a long way.* When you ask a guy a question, make eye contact but refrain from staring too intently into his eyes. Unless your relationship has advanced to the point where the question is "Are you taking me home to bed right now?" maintaining piercing eye contact might freak him out.

* ✳ *Be conversational.* You want to phrase your questions so you come off as friendly, not as the Gestapo.

* ✳ *Borrow from the Comedienne.* If you must be a smart-ass (and many Interrogator girls are) spin your questions so they translate into funny. A good example of this in a first-

meeting line would be to say, "Is all that really your hair? And here my girlfriend told me to look for the guy with the shaved head!"

If you fit into the Interrogator category, you've probably got some pretty decent verbal flirtation tactics in your arsenal already. And asking questions works really well with shy guys who don't have a lot of conversational gambits themselves. They appreciate a woman who knows how to keep the ball rolling, who won't let things hit a wall where there will be dead or dry spots. He figures that as long as she's asking questions, all he has to do is answer them in a way that finally gets her to ask the question he wants to hear—the question that will propel them into bed.

The Interrogator girl is usually quite self-confident. It takes a lot of bravado and chutzpah to ask strangers questions, and even more to keep a game face on when the questions don't get a response!

When you start up a conversation with a guy, try to ask more questions that he will answer with a yes than with a no. It doesn't matter what the subject matter is, but when a guy has said no to you three times in a row, it usually means he's telling you to back off.

The Shy Girl

It's really tough to talk to guys when you're shy . . . even guys you already know! Shy Girls often shy away from small talk because they're worried they won't have a single intelligent thing to say. They dread situations where they must meet new people. Being the center of attention makes them anxious. Sound familiar?

While other girls crave the limelight—it makes them want to run and hide! Shy Girls go out of their way to avoid any intensely focused attention. Strangely enough, although many a Shy Girl is drop-dead gorgeous, she hates it when people stare. While people who don't know them well read them as standoffish, Shy Girls are not really unfriendly. It's not that they don't like or enjoy other people. It's just that they prefer to fly under the radar. When you're a Shy Girl, it's painful to be in situations that require being chatty, because Shy Girls are rarely the bantering type.

But if you're a Shy Girl, don't fret. Believe it or not, the Shy Girl has a great advantage—men are drawn to a shy girl as bees are drawn to honey. Why? Because they love trying to draw her out. They see it as a challenge! Believe it or not, there are tons of guys out there who really go for the sexy, quiet type. Surely you've noticed (or you are) that silent, distant-seeming beauty at the party who just follows the conversation with her eyes? The woman who says very little is like a mountain men must climb. Their idea of getting to the top,—i.e., winning—is to get bring her out of her shell.

So if you're a Shy Girl, don't worry if you don't have a polished repertoire of witty dialogue ready to roll out at your next party. If talking really is painful, tiny scraps of dialogue, including the well-placed *yes*—or *maybe*, in a pinch—will suffice!

Top Tips for Shy Girls

* **Don't freak if you can't speak.** Just remember, no harm ever came from keeping your mouth shut. If words have tended to fail you, avoid them!

* **Bide your time!** If you're talking to a guy and can't think of anything to say right away, don't panic! Bide your

time with a smile—and don't forget to use your yeses and maybes. Eventually, he *will* say something that you can respond to. If any electricity, even the tiniest spark, occurs between two people, words aren't always necessary, at least not right away.

✳ **Shift into neutral.** To break a long or uncomfortable silence, try asking a guy a completely neutral question, like "Where do you think they keep the chips?" This is also a great line to use if you develop a sudden crush-at-first-sight thing after midnight at some out-of-the-way roadside 24-hour convenience store. Hey, happens all the time!

✳ **Keep it simple.** Many a love connection has gotten its start at a party when a Shy Girl asks a guy a simple question, such as "How long have you known the hostess?" That should get the ball rolling—and maybe even score you some juicy information!

✳ **Say no to mono**. If someone asks you a question, whatever you do, try not to answer in a monosyllable. One-word replies like yes, no, or um, don't give a guy much to latch on to, or cue him up for the next thing he could say. Even if your answer to his question can be answered in one word, try to expand on your yes or no answer by clarifying it. For example, if the question was, "Do you live around here?" Your answer could be, "No, but I'm only ten minutes away." That gives the guy fuel for his next question which might be, "Oh, really? Where?" But don't worry, Shy Girl. You don't have to say a mouthful. All you need to come up with is a response that leads to *his* asking you a question. In a pinch, ask him the same question he asked you!

Another advantage Shy Girls have over other women is that they're in that rare and lucky category of girls who can get away with sounding moony and romantic. Laughably romantic, in fact. At a wedding, when a Shy Girl whispers the words "Aren't they the most gorgeous couple," it's sweet and innocent. Hopeful. But coming from the Comedienne or the Interrogator, the words leave an entirely different impression.

Admitting that you're shy can be another great way to break the ice. Chalk it up to the thrill of the chase, but it never fails to incite male interest. Men will be drawn to you because they want to draw you out and cultivate your interest. And once you've got the guy hanging on your every sparsely delivered word, you get a chance to check them out and see if you want to get to know them better.

One last thing: If you're too shy to talk to a guy in person, try text-messaging him.

The Helper

The Helper has a giving spirit. She wants to help the guy understand himself better, help him comprehend what went wrong with his last relationship, delve into his psyche, get a grip on what is really going on between him and his mother. Ultimately the only thing that matters to the Helper is relationships—and she uses flirting as a means to this end. All the Helper really wants is for guys to face up to the fact that they probably need help—and she's just the one to give it!

The Helper tends to ask a lot of questions but, unlike the bold questioning ways of the Interrogator, her technique is much more touchy-feely. A Helper spends a great deal of time cultivating what might be known as a "safe zone" around her and the guy. She is expert at creating an emotional space the guy can slip into, where he feels comfortable discussing his emotions and problems, from work troubles to family issues to why he can't get his dog housebroken.

Helpers rely on simple psychological methods that real thera-pists use all the time, to get their flirt quarry to open up to them. Just as a therapist might do, they encourage an effect called "transference" to occur between them and a guy. In psychoanalysis, transference takes place over a period of weeks or months. In a bar or a club—or sitting on the steps outside a college dorm—this can happen almost instantly, especially after a couple of sour apple martinis.

The downside is that helpers tend to attract (and hold on to) guys who are really a bit messed up! Where other girls quickly suss out and dismiss guys who can't form real relationships, can't hold down a job, squabble constantly with their friends or who are a bad credit risk, the Helper has a tendency to fall into the trap of Ms. Fix-It, because she is so naturally sympathetic. She be-lieves that if she just gives this guy enough love and attention and her own special brand of advice, he'll come around and turn into Mr. Slightly-Flawed/Almost-Perfect. And maybe he will. But she also runs the risk of having a guy with a lot of problems now to-tally addicted to her. Yuck to that!

Top Tips for the Helper

* **Use your head.** Tilt your head when you're listening to a guy rail on about his problems. For some reason this makes you appear to be listening extra carefully.

* **Ask. Listen. Repeat.** Repeat back most of the same material content a guy says to you when he's in the mood for bitching and moaning. This is a therapeutic technique. For example, if the guy says, "I'm just so tired of her lying all the time," you say, "It's terrible to feel you're not being told the truth, isn't it?"

* **Express yourself.** Cultivate a sympathetic expression you can utter over and over. "How awful for you," usually works.

* **Get physical.** Offer hugs. Full body hugs have a way of turning into sexy embraces.

* **Curb your criticism.** Don't be a critical analyst—at least not right off the bat. Later, when you have him eating out of your hand, you can begin to address all his issues, which no doubt number in the dozens!

Men seem to melt for the Helper, and why not? She rarely talks about herself because her attention is focused on the guy. The Helper is kind, she's concerned, and she's an outstanding listener. She can feel the guy's pain. She also is a a back rubber, arm toucher, and hand stroker. A lot of of guys really dig that physical contact, especially when it's coming from a woman they barely know!

The Helper Hotline: There's a fine line between playing the Helper role and becoming stuck with a guy who seriously needs help. Check out these quick tips for telling the difference:

* Beware of a guy who *only* wants to tell you his problems. You want to flirt with him, not be his therapist!

* Moody guys can also be depressed guys. Do you really want to be a depressed guy's date?

* A guy who tells you that he really hates his mother is a guy to avoid. A guy who hates his mom doesn't really like women much. Besides, every girl he dates, he "turns into" his mother.
* If a guy has more baggage than you do, run for the hills. Hey, you've got your own problems, right?

Unless they're incredible actresses (and many women are), Helper girls truly are sympathetic people. They genuinely are concerned. If they aren't actually employed in one of the "helping" fields, usually they've had a fair amount of therapy themselves, which is where they've usually learned all their therapeutically flirtatious maneuvers in the first place! They also realize that other than eating, sleeping, and having sex, there's very little most men enjoy more than complaining about their job, their mother, their roommate, or their crazy ex-girlfriend who they claim won't stop stalking them. It's precisely this material that is the Helper girl's meat.

The Comedienne

We all know a Comedienne. She's the cut-up, the sassy one, the one who laughs at the drop of a dime. She's the girl you most like to spend time with even though she's also the one mostly likely to embarrass you! You never know what's going to come out of the Comedienne's mouth. She's completely unpredictable. That's part of her charm.

Comediennes principally come in two flavors. The first flavor is brash and bold and extroverted, whereas the other is wry, even self-deprecating, tending to direct the humor at herself. This doesn't mean that her conversational style is all about putting herself down; *au contraire*, she uses self-deprecation as a ploy to direct attention to herself!

Guys groove on girls who are funny because it takes the strain off their needing to be funny themselves. Funny girls are the life of a party, they're easy going, easy to get along with, more forgiving, and, best of all, they see the humor in nearly any situation, even awful ones. Funny girls are not uptight. Occasionally, they do get a bit loud and rowdy and small amounts of booze can set them off, loosening their tongues to the point where their friends just want to clap a hand over their mouth, but that can be fun, too. Imagine being out with a Comedienne at Chippendales!

Another major reason guys are drawn to funny girls is because funny girls often are superintelligent. There's a downside, though, as there are also lots of guys who are intimidated or rattled by this kind of girl.

If you're a Comedienne, then you probably already know that if you happen upon a guy who truly enjoys you, it can turn into kismet. You turn into an instant tag team—he can play the straight man to your funny girl. Or you can pair up to form your own comedy team. Classic screwball comedies depend on these couplings! Comediennes are very attractive to many types of men: Shy guys love them because it means they don't have to be the one who is "on." Socially confident men admire them because they appreciate the funny girl's ballsiness. Intellectual guys adore them because true wit is a sign of great intelligence.

There is such a thing as being *too* funny, however. The Comedienne has to beware of becoming too biting, too barbed, too pointed. While funny lines and jokes can set a tone or perk up an otherwise boring evening, cruel humor hurts people's feelings.

Therefore, the Comedienne must take care not to create an at-mosphere of hostility—even if it seems funny at the time. Mean-spirited humor has a way of coming back to haunt the joke-teller and bite her on the ass. In a movie, it's hilarious when a sexy woman humorously destroys some poor schnook, but in real life men perceive a woman who behaves this way as a bitch.

Top Tips for Comediennes

* **Be upbeat!** Use your humor to do people good, not put them down or destroy them
* **Be prepared.** Develop a repertoire of jokes you can tell in a number of situations. G-rated humor is always welcome, although you should have a few off-color ones at your fingertips. There's a time and a place when non-PC humor really works, but your instinct has to be pitch perfect to know when it's okay to tell a dirty joke. Avoid falling into the trap of relying on bathroom humor to get you through an evening unless you're attending a frat party or a roast, in which case, babe, just go for it. Here's a hint: Have an animal sex joke ready. For some strange reason, men in groups always love them!
* **Find strength in numbers.** If you are telling jokes, don't stop at one. Three jokes in a row are optimal, espe-cially if they're short ones. The reason for multiple jokes is simple. Usually it takes more than one joke to get people laughing. That's why professional comics tell groups of jokes. Also once you get people laughing, they like to continue the laugh. Whatever you do, avoid telling one long-winded, many-layered joke. Not only are they hard

to remember and tell, but they're almost impossible to hear in bars or crowds.

* **Borrow, if necessary.** Don't worry if you don't have a lot of original material. You don't have to be the joke writer to deliver the lines. Steal funny things to say from whoever and wherever. If you get your best material from books like this one, your words won't be recognized as quickly as ones you steal from a hit movie.

* **Get physical.** You don't have to be verbally funny all of the time. Physical humor works excellently in certain situations. For example, there's nothing funnier than an attractive woman who makes her point by rolling her eyes.

* **Laugh at yourself.** If something funny happens to you, make a joke about it. Guys love women who know how to laugh at themselves.

The Comedienne's advantages are myriad. For one thing, women and men alike want to hang out with her, as she's got a natural appeal that can turn any gathering into an event.

No matter what, the Comedienne must know when, where, and how to wield her charm. In very public situations, she might opt to keep a low profile and only shower the full force of her humor privately on a special guy or friend. Or she may save her humorous take on a scene or situation for a blow-by-blow dissection later on e-mail. The one sure thing about a funny girl is, if she's really funny, it will come out no matter what the situation!

No matter how naturally funny you are, in certain social situations it's better to honor standard, straitlaced social decorum. That means no cracking jokes at funerals, okay?

FLIRTING—IT'S IN THE STARS

Just for fun, see how these astrological signposts dovetail with your personal flirting style!

Aquarius Girls (January 20–February 18) hate to budge. When they fix their sights on their quarry, they stop at nothing in their pursuit of him!

Pisces Girls (February 19–March 20), while very shy, are expert mimics. Adept at mirroring the exact speech and mannerisms of any guy they're talking to, they use this tool to reel guys in.

Aries Girls (March 21–April 19) are antsy and restless. When it comes to men, they like to keep it moving!

Taurus Girls (April 20–May 20) are notoriously stubborn. When they fixate on a guy, they like to keep on working it until he gives in!

Gemini Girls (May 21–June 20) are natural chatterboxes. They have very clever tongues that they like to use to tie a guy up in knots!

Cancer Girls (June 21–July 22) have the special ability of knowing how to make total strangers feel like members of their family. Watch out, however, for that famous Cancerian moodiness!

Leo Girls (July 23–August 22) are, um, formidable. They can also be very stubborn and don't like it one bit when they don't get their way!

Virgo Girls (August 23–September 22) are experts at disguising their vulnerability by lavishly praising others—or criticizing them unmercifully!

Libra Girls (September 23–October 22) are natural nurturers. They also will go far out of their way to avoid confrontations!

Scorpio Girls (October 23–November 21) are naturally provocative and sexy. They're also pillars of emotional strength even if they sometimes fruitlessly cling to their romantic attachments.

Sagittarius Girls (November 22–December 21) are super-adaptable, which means they can mutate into being whatever kind of girl the situation requires. They're also party animals who are usually the last to leave a scene.

Capricorn Girls (December 23–January 19) are very determined and like to set goals for themselves. What they have to watch out for is remembering that the end doesn't always justify the means!

Chapter Two

The Flirtspeak 5

What's the first thing a man usually notices about a woman? Unless he has the opportunity to hear her voice or read her words first, it's her body and her face that form his initial opinion. Undeniably, having a slammin' body and knowing how to use it are no-brainer tactics to attracting a man. That's the reason why so many women spend a fortune on bras that exaggerate or create cleavage, and on clothing that firms and tightens and tucks. But just as body image and language telegraphs a message, so do the words that come out of your mouth—and while wearing revealing clothing or swishing your hips may catch a guy's attention initially, it's the words you use that will determine whether or not he sticks around.

Additionally, in these cyber-crazed days, you're just as likely to meet someone on the Internet and then "talk" to them on the computer before meeting them in person, which means that it's more important than ever for you to learn that there is a "come-hither" verbal vocabulary that is just as powerful as any language you express with your body. In the exact same way you might find yourself standing up straighter, tucking in your tummy, or flipping your hair to catch a man's eye, there are words you can say to grab a man's interest—and keep him interested. So, if you've never been much of a body language flirt, or if you're not especially comfortable with your body, you can make flirting with words your ultimate secret weapon—and the Flirtspeak 5 is your key to flirting success.

The Flirtspeak 5

In journalism, Who, What, When, Where, and Why, or the Five Ws, are standard questions any good reporter asks when she is reporting a story. That means assessing who was involved, what happened, when it happened, where it happened, and why it happened. The exact same thinking holds true when you're forming opening lines and developing conversation—we call it the Flirtspeak 5. It's the same basic principles of journalism—applied to flirting:

* Who you're talking to
* What you're talking about
* When the conversation occurs and its duration
* Where the conversation happens
* Why you're talking in the first place

Aside from mastering the simple art of hello (which we'll get to soon enough), knowing the Flirtspeak 5 by heart is your most indispensable tool. Despite its name, you can use the Flirtspeak 5 for much more than flirtations. At the most introductory level, most conversation-starters and icebreakers are beyond gender, so you can put these tips to use in any number of situations—from interviews to work functions to any other event that requires you to make sparkling, witty small talk.

Who

Let's begin at the beginning, shall we? When entering any social situation, first assess the room and decide who you should talk to.

Who you should talk to is often a matter of circumstance. Naturally, you'll want to talk to anyone you find cute, anyone who can advance your career, anyone who can help open doors for you. That guy who seems all thumbs one machine over at the copy shop? He could be your next boyfriend. Or boss! Maybe there *is* a reason why you're both spending Saturday night at Kinko's!

If you're in a party situation, the "who" may be a little bit different. You might want to approach someone you already know. Or, if you spy a cute guy standing alone across the room—go for it!

What

Okay, so you've chosen your flirt quarry du jour. Now, what are you going to talk about? Weather is probably the easiest and most obvious choice. The reason? Everyone can talk about the weather. You can talk about how hot it is, how cold, how much snow there's been, how much you love the fall, the spring, the summer. If the conversation is going well and you feel comfortable, you may even want to drop in a funny weather anecdote—like the time you got snowed into a cabin way out in the middle of nowhere with no company at all save the passing ice fisherman who stayed up with you all night, playing poker. Okay, so that's a fictional example, although it does make for a provocative story. Feel free to borrow it and make good use of it—all's fair in flirting!

Other good things to talk about are food, pets, travel destinations, headlines. People say you should never discuss politics or religion at a party but sometimes they make the best topics, depending on the company you're in. Basically, anything you have an opinion on is fodder for conversation or at least as a conversation starter. If it turns out your opinion on something is diametrically opposed to that of your new acquaintance—for example, you're a conservative who rapidly finds herself developing a crush on a Democrat—you can always engage in a friendly debate. What do you think Maria Shriver first talked about when she met Arnold Schwarzenegger?

A few words about gossip

Gossip is fun, but it can also blow up in your face!

To be safe, stick to what might be called "public gossip": stuff about celebrities, politicians, whatever juicy tidbits have already made the national gossip columns in newspapers and magazines. Anything you can pull off *Entertainment Tonight* is also safe for spreading. On a more local level, while it may be tempting to dish about your biggest rival (say, strategically letting it drop to a major blabbermouth that so-and-so has herpes?), remember that what goes around, comes around, and you may be the next target of malicious rumor-mongering!

DO'S AND DON'TS FOR GOOD GOSSIPING

Do spread good gossip about yourself. There's a very thin line between news and gossip when it pertains to yourself. Got a great new job or discovered a hot new club? Promote it!

Don't tell tales on your friends.

Don't tattle. It's so middle school.

Do crush nasty gossip about people you know that comes your way. Just say, "That is so not true," and then close your lips!

Don't hesitate to say, "Is that gossip?" when you want to squelch some. Accompany this statement with a withering glance.

Don't gossip at the water cooler or in the bathrooms at work. Save any juicy stuff that comes up at work for the margarita happy hour!

Do smile when you hear something juicy about your worst enemy or arch rival. Just don't contribute!

In the end, what you talk about the first time you're meeting someone doesn't really matter. What counts is that you spoke. It's true that there will be times when you won't get a chance to make a second impression (assuming that you bombed the first), but odds are that if you didn't click at all with a guy on the first meeting, you probably weren't meant to flirt with him anyway. Struck out? Move on!

When

Timing is everything—especially when it comes to the fine art of flirty conversation. Finding the right moment to open your mouth can make or break any encounter.

For example, if the guy you've been eyeing from across the room is having a heated cell phone conversation, it's probably not a great time to approach him and start gabbing away. But if you spot him hanging out near the bean dip and twiddling his thumbs, then you can seize the opportunity for a flirtatious exchange.

Breaking the barrier—how to work your way into a group conversation to get his attention

The "when" changes slightly if you're trying to break into a group conversation. So how do you gracefully get in there and turn the high beams of his attention on to *you?* Wait and listen for a few minutes before making any comments.

* If you approach a group (even a group of two) of people who are already talking, don't barge right in.

* Don't say anything at first. Give him a chance to get a good look at you. Try to pick up the thread of the conversation before offering any comment. In other words, keep your mouth shut until you find a topic on which you can base a question or comment.

* When you do speak, it has to be something witty, something pithy, something grabby. If the only thing you can think to say is "Um," don't say anything. Yet.

* If the opportunity to slip in an aside to the guy occurs, speak directly into his ear. You don't have to whisper and make it look like you're putting the rest of the group on Mute. Just speak to him and him alone . . . but only if it seems like everybody else is engrossed in the conversation.

* If he speaks to you first, you know you're in.

* If he asks you to separate off from the group, go with him. The next thing that can happen is that you'll get a chance to speak alone with him. And that's a score! The only time it's safe to use the "interruption" method of breaking into a group is if you've just heard an incredible piece of gossip or some other delicious dirt that you just have to share. But be aware

that your interruption will cause you to be the center of attention, so if you're not ready for the spotlight, don't enter it!

Where

Of all of the five Ws, "where" is probably the easiest. Once you begin thinking of opportunities for talking to men, suddenly they spring up everywhere: at work, the health club, waiting in any line, the coffee bar, buying a newspaper, on public transportation, in a supermarket, by the gas pump, at the Laundromat. In other words, wherever!

Try one of these openers—they're practically foolproof:

* At the office: "Happy Monday. If any Monday can ever really be 'happy.'"
* By the mailboxes in your apartment building: "How was your weekend?"
* At the Laundromat: "I'm all out of change. Can you break this single?"
* On the street in town: "Do you know if they ticket you here much?"
* At a café or a lunch counter: "Do you know if this seat is taken?"

Why

In any situation where you've made the decision to speak, it's a good idea to ask yourself why you're bothering. Purpose is critical to any successful dialogue. In fact it should be the thing that drives your conversation, that gives it meaning.

Your purpose in starting a flirtatious conversation could be any one of the following:

* You think he's hot.
* You know who he is and hope he can get you a better job.
* You used to date his roommate.
* You're bored and he's the only other human being in the vicinity.

Flirty Tip: *Definitely talk to guys just because you're bored. It's a great way to practice your flirt skills with no strings attached!*

Volume Control

You might be surprised to know that how loudly or softly you speak, er, speaks volumes beyond your actual words. Did you know that the more softly you speak, the more closely others have to get near you to listen? While the girl with the boom-box voice initially grabs all the attention, often it's the chick who speaks very softly who holds the attention of the guy.

Using Your Voice Like a Body Part

You know how you can flex your bicep to make it look big and strong? Shake your booty to call a man's attention to it? You can do the same thing with your voice. Treat it for what it is: a movable, working part.

Imagine your voice is a warm and cozy arm that you can wrap around a guy. Make it purr. Or visualize it as a pair of strong legs that are carrying you to a destination. Or a heart beating a tattoo drumroll inside your chest. When you recognize that your voice is an instrument, you open up the possibilities of all the ways that you can play it to create musical harmony with a man.

Need some examples? Take a tip from professional dog trainers, who use a commanding tone to get a dog to do their bidding. Try saying "Down, boy!" as though you mean it. Or use a coaxing tone to prod a reluctant guy along. Try saying, "Why don't you join me on the dance floor?" to the cute guy you just met at your nephew's bar mitzvah. Flex your vocal muscles! Try saying, "And your name is . . . ?" in a playful tone, then in an inquisitive tone and finally in a seductive tone. See how it sounds different each time?

Turning It Down and Pumping It Up

Every woman has a natural volume at which she speaks. The Comedienne may be the loudest person in the room; the Shy Girl may not get above a whisper, even at her loudest.

A lot of women also have a tendency to raise their voice when they're feeling anxious. Unconsciously, many women think that if they don't have much to say, it'll sound better if what comes out is at peak volume. This is almost always a mistake. If you're really anxious about what's going to come out of your mouth, a much better policy is just to say less—and keep what you're saying sotto voce, which is Italian for "quiet voice." That way, if you say the wrong thing, the less likely the chances that any guy will hear it!

Now you know when to keep your voice down and when it's okay to get a little crazy, but did you know that you can *also* play with your volume level to change the tone of a situation or imply a flirtatious attitude? Let's examine the phrase "It's time for me to go home now." Think about using this phrase in the following situations, and how the implication is different for each:

* A loud party
* At your best friend's house, when five other people are over and three of them are guys
* At your cousin's wedding
* At your boyfriend's apartment after a particularly romantic date

What's in a Whisper?

You got punished for it in grade school, and it's frowned upon at work, but when you're out on the flirting prowl, whispering can be a very powerful tool. Whispering by its very nature is very intimate. Why? There's something really sensual about mouth-ear connection. You can actually feel the whisperer's hot breath on your ear, which is thrilling and forbidden.

The magic of whispering is that it immediately creates a society of two that cultivates an atmosphere of intimacy, closeness, a bond. Anyone you've ever shared a whisper with is accorded the title of confidante, a French word used to describe a very special, very intimate sort of friend.

Just as you can alter the volume of your regular voice, you can play with your whisper to suit a certain situation. If you're going for the playful approach, using a louder whisper gets you close to the guy without seeming too obvious. And if you're going for sweet and sexy, then lean in close and let your voice become sensual and wispy.

And since imitation is the sincerest form of flattery, why not borrow the whisper tactics of your favorite Hollywood heroines? Here are some great examples of whispering styles you can emulate.

The Notebook: This entire movie is rich with whispering. The two whisperers are Rachel McAdams and Ryan Gosling. In one scene Ryan takes Rachel out for the first time. They're walking in the middle of the street and then suddenly they just lie down together in the middle of the street. It's such a bonding moment when they're lying together . . . whispering.

The Matrix: Keanu Reeves and Carrie-Anne Moss are in a club and she's trying to explain to him—whispering in his ear—what a matrix is.

Say Anything: John Cusack and Ione Skye are in his car and they've just made love for the first time. Peter Gabriel's song "In Your Eyes" is on, and the two of them look at each other and she whispers, "I like this song." He looks into her eyes as if he really gets her and they kiss and kiss and it's the real thing, a real in-love kiss.

Wedding Date: Debra Messing pays Dermot Mulroney, a professional male escort/prostitute, $6,000 to fly to London with her and be her date at a wedding where her ex-fiancé is the best man. Dermot whispers hot stuff in Debra's ear to bolster her confidence and, when he's finished, she says, "You are good."

DO'S AND DON'TS OF WHISPERING

Do cultivate a sexy, breathy whisper. Just don't overdue it. You don't want him to think you're asthmatic!

Don't whisper sexily in a man's ear unless you mean business—there's flirting and then there's leading him on.

Do smile when you whisper. Not a broad, teeth-baring grin. Try channeling your inner Mona Lisa.

Don't whisper things that are pure gossip . . . unless an item is just too juicy a tidbit to pass up.

Do whisper sentences that contain words that are body parts. The word "thigh," for example, is so much sexier when it's spoken sotto voce.

Don't whisper more than a few words at a time. Long-winded whispering is really tiresome.

Do whisper when you want to set up an immediate alchemy of intimacy. Even just one hastily whispered phrase can produce intense special effects!

Don't spit. Whispering is cute. Spraying saliva isn't.

Do have fresh breath when you're whispering. Always carry breath mints, and avoid whispering if you've just scarfed down a big bowl of linguine with clam sauce.

Flirty Tip: *Speaking first and speaking smart is empowering, but having too much power can be a bad thing!*

Vocally Playin' Possum

Believe it or not, there are times when slurring your words can actually work to your advantage! Of course if you've been at happy hour and you've already downed two sour apple martinis, chances are you're a bit slurry even if you don't want to be. So why would you ever want to make it appear that you're not quite fully capable of fully enunciating? Because, while it may be a sneaky tactic, it can often help you get the upper hand in the conversation.

Hence, the term "playin' possum."

Just as an opossum will "play dead" to get its enemies to leave it alone and go away, a female who pretends to be just a tiny bit wasted (and the quickest way to do that is to slur a few words) can quickly gain access to what kind of guy he really is. Think about it—if he thinks you're a little out of it, he may be more likely to reveal his true colors. For example, is he a nice guy who wants to take care of you? Or is he a jerk who sees a little bit of tipsiness as a way to take advantage? Will he make it his business to know you've got a safe ride home (because friends don't let friends drink and drive) or will he tell the bartender to pour you another?

Another good reason to occasionally slur (or drop) a word is to get a guy to move closer. If he can't understand you, he'll move closer to hear what you've been saying. As he sidles up beside you so that the two of you are mere inches away—in other words, when you've really got his ear—enunciate. This might be a good time to say something deliciously double entendre such as, "It's awfully warm in here, isn't it?"

WHICH MOVIE STAR FLIRT ARE YOU?

Take this test to find out which star's flirt style is most like yours

1. **Which scenario most describes your idea of a perfect date?**
   a. Candlelight dinner à deux
   b. Theme park
   c. Rollerblading
   d. Rock concert
   e. Dinner and a movie
   f. Take out Chinese at home with your boyfriend

2. What is your favorite type of music?
   a. Hard rock
   b. Alternative
   c. Soft rock
   d. Classical
   e. Christian
   f. Jazz

3. What is your favorite kind of movie?
   a. Comedy
   b. Horror
   c. Musical
   d. Romance
   e. Documentary
   f. Mystery

4. Which job would you choose if you could only choose one?
   a. Stewardess
   b. Professional tennis star
   c. Schoolteacher
   d. Police officer
   e. Bartender
   f. CEO of your own company

5. If you had an hour to kill, how would you spend it?
   a. At the gym
   b. Fooling around with your boyfriend
   c. Channel surfing
   d. Listening to the radio

e. Sleeping

f. Reading

6. Which of the following is your favorite color?

a. Yellow

b. White

c. Sky blue

d. Teal

e. Gold

f. Red

7. If it could magically appear before you, which food would you eat right now?

a. Chocolate cake

b. Margarita pizza

c. California roll sushi

d. Penne vodka

e. Caesar salad

f. King crab

8. Which is your favorite holiday?

a. Halloween

b. Christmas

c. New Year's

d. Valentine's Day

e. Thanksgiving

f. Fourth of July

9. If you could travel anywhere, where would it be?

a. Aspen

b. Venice

   c. Atlantic City

   d. Maui

   e. Hollywood

   f. Vancouver

10. Who would you rather spend time with?

   a. An intellectual

   b. A beautiful person

   c. A party animal

   d. Someone who is perpetually optimistic

   e. Someone who is laughs (and cries) at the drop of a hat

   f. Someone who has it all together personally and professionally

Total up your points on each question:

1. a–4 b–2 c–5 d–1 e–3 f–6
2. a–2 b–1 c–4 d–5 e–3 f–6
3. a–2 b–1 c–3 d–4 e–5 f–6
4. a–4 b–5 c–3 d–2 e–1 f–6
5. a–5 b–4 c–2 d–1 e–3 f–6
6. a–1 b–5 c–3 d–2 e–4 f–6
7. a–3 b–2 c–1 d–4 e–5 f–6
8. a–1 b–3 c–2 d–4 e–5 f–6
9. a–4 b–5 c–1 d–4 e–3 f–6
10. a–5 b–2 c–1 d–3 e–4 f–6

35

How you scored and what it all means:

(10–17 points) You are Angelina Jolie.

You're the wild and crazy one, and you know it! You are very fun loving, but you have been known to take your fun to extremes. You know what you are doing, though, and are much in control of your own life. Some people may raise an eyebrow at the way you lead your life, but you have your beliefs and you stick to them! Do know that your wild-child spirit will draw men to you, but you might scare away female friends.

(18–26 points) You are Katie Holmes.

You are fun, friendly, and popular! You are a real crowd-pleaser. You have probably been out on the town your share of times, yet you come home with the values that your mother taught you. Marriage and children are very important to you, but only after you have had your fill of the fun single-girl lifestyle. Make sure the man you settle down with is a good one because you're the kind of gal who may just mate for life!

(27–34 points) You are Jennifer Aniston.

You are cute, and everyone loves you. Your friends would go to the wall for you and you'd do the same for them. You've never deliberately hurt anyone else's feelings, although there have been times that others have hurt yours. You are the kind of woman who is lucky in life. Steer clear of gorgeous bad boys like Brad Pitt and your life will be a breeze.

(35–42 points) You are Diane Lane.

You are a talented, beautiful, romantic. You're a real lover. You know how to enjoy the simple but elegant moments in life. Despite your incredible charisma, deep down you are a serious individual with real commitments and goals. You are family oriented so steer clear of handsome playboys. They're not worthy of you and they'll only disappoint!

(43–50 points) You are Julianne Moore.

You are brilliant, a real thinker. You approach every situation with a game plan. You honor your body and don't do things to contaminate or injure it. You are careful who you associate with and what you put in your mouth. You are nobody's fool or their doormat, either. You're very particular about who you let be your friend. When you do decide to settle down, you will choose a mate who is worthy of you. With your feet firmly planted on the ground (even in stilettos), you aren't easily taken in by superficial guys. Your standards for a man are high and you're proud of that!

(51–60 points) You are Nicole Kidman.

You are awesome. You are beautiful and talented and, even when bad things happen to you, you manage to make it seem as though you're unscathed. It takes hard work and perseverance to make your life appear so smooth, but it's important to you that a calm and collected exterior is what other people see. You are very picky when it comes to men because you've had your heart broken a time or two, but that hasn't closed your heart or stopped you from being open to love.

Chapter Three

Taking the Plunge

At this point no doubt you are champing at the bit to get out there and start flirting . . . er, talking! This chapter will provide you with useful tips on how to verbally conduct yourself around guys in normal, real-life situations . . . and how to fine-tune and play with what you say to give you the full court advantage.

It All Starts with "Hi"

So now you know who to approach, what to say, when to say it, where to say it, and why you're doing it. But how the heck do you get started? It all begins with that silly little two-letter word we so often take for granted—"hi".

Saying hello is the easiest (not to mention the most obvious) way to approach a guy. It really *is* that simple. You don't have to be particularly brilliant or witty—you just have to break the ice. And unless you're dealing with a complete dud, he *will* respond to you!

Even though it's just one word, "Hi" is really *the* all-important opening line, and it will set the tone for the rest of your conversation. If you're a minimalist, you can just go in for the "hi" and see what happens from there. But there are a couple of standard variations that work just as well as springboards for conversation. Check out these five easy openers:

1. **"Hello."**
2. **"Hey, I've seen you around."**
3. **"I'm lost."**
4. **"You look lost."**
5. **"What time does this thing get started?"**

Now let's examine what makes these lines work.

"Hello"

"Hello" is the easiest thing you can say to any one, including strangers! "Hello" is friendly. "Hello" is no commitment. "Hello" gives the other person something easy to say in return. All they have to say back is "Hello," and—hello?! You're talking!

"Don't I Know You from Somewhere?"

This is a great line to use, even if it's not entirely truthful. This line works because it instantly telegraphs the message that you've had your eye on this guy. You're putting it right out there that you already noticed him. How flattering to his ego is that? Most importantly, "I've seen you around," suggests a kind of instant karma or familiarity. It's a way of saying that even though the two of you have never shared the spoken word, nonetheless you're connected. The line is also bold without being aggressive—and plenty of guys are turned on by boldness.

"You Look Lost"

This is a helpful yet provocative comment to make to a man in nearly any situation. With this comment, it's all about the subtext. Different approaches will yield different results. You can use several different types of approach with this statement, depending on the tone of your voice, because it's all about the subtext. For instance, you might try the innocent approach—a kind and gentle soul offering help and direction. Or you can go with the sly, sassy approach—even if the fragile male ego, you might recall, rarely permits him to admit this. Saying "You look lost," to a man sounds almost like a challenge . . . but a challenge he'll enjoy rising to. In the best-case scenario, the guy will admit that he's lost and let you lead him around . . . by your little finger.

"I'm Lost"

Announcing that *you* are lost is even better because it gives him a reason to help you. Lost girls need help, and men really love when they get an opportunity to spring to assistance. Also, once he tells you where you are or how to get to where you're going, he might even offer to personally escort you there. Say yes!

"What Time Does This Thing Get Started?"

This is an incredibly useful line that can be applied in myriad situations. Trot it out as an icebreaker while you're waiting for an event to begin—from a ball game to a work function—even in front of the movie theater. It matters not a whit what time the function *actually* begins—it's just a way to strike up a conversation. Or you can use it on a guy you've been chatting up at an otherwise dull party, and you're clearly letting him know that you're open to getting to know him a little better.

Creating a Signature Opening Line

Once you've built up an arsenal of standard openers you're comfortable using, you may want to consider spicing up your repertoire by creating your own signature opening line—something that makes a strong first impression and sets you apart from everyone else.

Your signature opener is an all-use, all-occasion collection of words that can be used in just about any situation. A signature opening line also can be very personal. It can be something that really tells a guy something about you, something indicative of your true personality.

Actress /playwright/ comedienne Mae West, who was known for her sense of humor, her figure, and her sexiness, made famous her great line, "Is that a pistol in your pocket or are you just glad to see me?" Mae's quips were always a tad outrageous. Your signature opening line doesn't have to be as forward as something the great star might have said, but if you are going to develop a signature opening line, make sure it's memorable.

To create your own great signature opening line, the one that gets you smoothly into the social swim, first determine what your flirtstyle personality is:

* If you're a Smooth Talker, the trick is to sound slick but not insincere. A complimentary line like "What is that cologne? You smell delicious," is effective but harmless.

* If you're a Ditz, you can get away with murder . . . almost. "I would have been here an hour ago except I had to catch the cat," is effective. At the very least it'll get the guy asking you all about the cat. (Note: you don't actually have to have a cat.)

* If you're an Interrogator girl, you'll want to lead with a question. "And you are . . . ?" is a good start.

* If you're a Shy Girl capitalize on it. Your best line might be to say, "I'm shy."

* If you're a Helper girl, you always sound concerned. "Are you having fun yet?" works well in most scenarios.

* If you're a Comedienne, say something funny, like, "Hi, I'm Leslie. Wanna lick my eyebrows?"

Play the Name Game

Once you've charmed him with your witty opener, another big part of endearing yourself to a man (or for that matter, anyone) is that you remember his name. Recalling someone's name can be tricky—especially in a social situation when things are happening quickly. And with so much competition out there, remembering the names of the men you meet really makes a difference. Imagine how embarrassed you'll feel if you keep running into that amazing guy all over town but for the life of you, you can't remember if his name is Eamon or Aaron.

But the Name Game isn't just the key to dating. It's also a fantastic tool for just work or business situations as well. By playing the Name Game, you increase your skills as a master networker—and these days, it's all about networking. You know what they say—it's not only *what* you know, it's *who* you know. In a business situation, being able to recall a name at a moment's notice can make the difference between your being a girl with a *job* and a girl with a *career*.

Tips for Remembering People's Names

✧ Repeat his name as soon as you've heard it. If the guy says "I'm Will," you say, "Hi, Will."

✧ Use his name as frequently as possible in your next five utterances. That way it'll become imprinted and fixed in your mind.

✧ If you're especially bad with names, try escaping to the restroom for a moment and write his name down somewhere. Try not to lose that scrap of paper!

✧ If he gives you his business card, read it before you stow it. Say his name exactly the way it's printed on the card. So if his card says his name is Benjamin, call him Benjamin until he tells you he'd really prefer you call him Ben.

✧ If his last name is easier to remember than his first, just call him by that name. Calling a guy by his last name is sexier, anyway.

✧ Fumbled his name? Here's how to handle it:

  ◆ Apologize! Men love it when women say, I'm sorry!
  ◆ Repeat his name back to him three times, like, "Nick, Nick, Nick." Then say, "Now I won't forget." Smile sexily.
  ◆ Say, "Oh, it's James? Oooh, I just love that name."

EASY OPENERS TO USE IN EVERYDAY SITUATIONS

✳ At the airport when the shuttle you hoped to take never shows up: "Want to split a taxi?"

✳ In line at the coffee bar: "I hear they make a great soy latté."

✳ In the grocery aisle: "Where do they keep the cocktail mixes?"

✳ In the food court at the mall: "Can we share this table? I'm sorry to intrude but it's just so crowded."

✳ At the Laundromat: "Oops, I forgot to bring any detergent. Do you think I could borrow yours?"

ADAPT YOUR FIRST LINE TO YOUR FLIRTSTYLE

Smooth Talker: "You look at me so strangely"
Ditz: "Did I just bump into you? Or did you just bump into me?"
Interrogator: "You look like you're waiting for somebody."
Shy Girl: "Am I too early?"
Helper: "You look like you're having a bad day."
Comedienne: "Over here!"

DO TALK TO STRANGERS!

If you really heed all your mother's advice, and never, ever, talk to strangers, frankly, you miss out on a lot. While it's common sense to steer clear of any man who is lurking, leering, obviously letching, or doing anything weird with his hands, it's important to remember that not all strangers are dangerous creeps who dream only of molesting you.

There are many excellent reasons why young girls and young women should not approach strange men. But when a big girl sees a man she wants to talk to, she talks to him!

How to Handle Different Types of Guys

All guys, unfortunately, are not created equal. Sure, they're the same species and what they share in common is an abundance of testosterone, but no matter how great your cache of great opening lines may be, you might have to dig deep in your toolbox to find the right line to match the right guy. So before we go any further, here's the skinny on how to break the ice with each kind of guy.

The Shy Guy

He's easy prey for savvy girl flirts. And he's such an easy read because his body language gives him away every time. His posture alone will inform you he's shy before he's opened his mouth. It's fairly easy to spot the Shy Guy—he's the one with his hands shoved in his pockets or he's hunched over in a slouch. Or he could be standing ramrod stiff, his heart beating wildly under his lumberjack shirt just because you're looking at him.

You have to approach a Shy Guy pretty carefully. He's easily scared off. Try a little bit of Interrogator mode mixed with a bit of the Shy Girl when you approach him—this will help you draw him out without coming off as too aggressive. It'll make him feel safer if he thinks you're kind of shy yourself. Any direct come-on, physical or verbal, will send him galloping off into the sunset—alone—so it's best if you take a sideways kind of approach with him.

The first thing to do with a Shy Guy is touch him. The point is to break the tension and put him at ease. (Of course, paradoxically, your touch will both calm and excite . . . any time a woman touches a man, she's exciting him.) Your touch should be friendly and unassuming. Put your hand on his arm. Briefly touch his sleeve. But don't go overboard with the touching right away.

When you speak to a Shy Guy, keep the message simple, but try to avoid asking yes or no questions, because it's nearly impossible to draw him out that way.

Good icebreakers to try on Shy Guys are:

* "Hi. What do you think of . . . ?"
* "Great weather, isn't it?"
* "That's the cutest dog. Where did you find him?"
* "Do you know how late this place stays open?"
* "Is this seat taken or is it okay if I grab it?"

The Alpha Guy

The Alpha Guy is the one most women are drawn to. Heck, most men are drawn to him, too. Alpha Guys are "guy's guys." They're supermasculine and ballsy, yet they take pride in their appearance, and are usually carefully groomed—even if their look is Brad Pitt messy. They're the guys with great jobs, great cars, the great apartment in the city or the grand country house. The Alpha Guy often travels with a little entourage of friends around him whose main job is to remind him that he's the Alpha Guy.

Unlike the Shy Guy, Alpha Guys can handle the direct approach, so don't be afraid to break out a little of the Smooth Talker when you approach him. In fact, some of them demand it and automatically think less of any woman who doesn't at least make a play for the upper hand.

There are really only two good ways to break the ice with an Alpha Guy:

1. **Take on an Alpha Girl persona yourself and impress him with your witty banter and Smooth Talker ways, or**

2. **Play the opposite game and play passive to his aggressive. You have to be the yin to his yang.**

The trouble is that you don't know, going in, which kind of girl this particular guy most is drawn to until you've further sussed him out. That's why channeling a little bit of the Comedienne or the Ditz is often the fastest way in to opening the Alpha Guy's notoriously chilly heart. Funny is warm but it's neutral. And it gives you both something to talk about.

Some great first things to say to an Alpha Guy might be:

* (Looking at his hat) "I think your head is even bigger than mine."
* (At a club or party) "If I take off my stilettos, would that make you the tallest person here?"
* (At an office event) "I either need a bigger desk or a smaller computer. What about you?"

One last tip: Always manage to get the "you" word into any first communication with an Alpha Guy. To put it bluntly, his ego requires it.

The Goofy Guy

The Goofy Guy is fun—but beware. He can go from adorable to annoying in under five minutes, so you want to approach this guy with caution.

An adorably goofy guy is very cute, very sweet, and very clumsy. He's can be clumsy in his speech (always manages to say the exactly wrong thing) or his actions (could be a spiller). Even though he's the guy who will step on your foot, trip down the stairs, spill his drink, ruin the punchline of any joke, or say the exactly wrong thing at exactly the wrong time (he'll be the guy who mistakes your sister for your mother), there's something so charming and sweet about him that you just have to forgive him. So how can you tell the difference between a Goof (adorable) and a Goofus (annoying)? You can't, because it's strictly a matter of personal taste. Actually, it all boils down to pheromones. If you have a chemical attraction to this guy, it won't matter that he can't keep his socks up. On the other hand, he could be the most adorable goof in the world, but if his scent glands don't flare your nostrils, the next time he spills his drink on you, you're gonna holler.

How to Tell a Goof from a Goofus

He's a goof if at first he keeps flubbing your first name.
He's a goofus if after the third time you've pronounced it, he still can't get it right.

He's a goof if he goes to fetch you a fresh drink and brings you the wrong one.
He's a goofus if he says he's going to bring you a drink and then never brings it.

He's a goof if you ask him to hold your dog and, when you come back, the leash is wound around his feet but he's on his knees on the ground and the dog is kissing him.

He's a goofus if you ask him to hold your dog and when you come back he says, "What dog?"

The way to approach a goofy guy is to be the antithesis of goofy. The one thing a goofy guy instinctually understands he doesn't need is a woman who is goofy. That's why a woman who seems together, who seems in control, a woman with a sense of direction, a woman who is *helpful* is, for him, so desirable.

If you really like this guy, channel your inner Interrogator or your Helpful girl style. Goofy guys are already pretty funny so they don't really need (or want) a Comedienne. And if your natural style is Ditz, forget about it—you're just too two-peas-in-a-pod to make it work.

Some good things to say right away to a goofy man are:

✳   (In a buffet line) "You look like you could use a little help with that plate."

✳   (Anywhere) "You've got a smudge on your forehead and it isn't even Ash Wednesday. Mind if I wipe it off?"

✳   (In any parking lot—preferably during the day!) You can't remember where you parked your car? That's so funny. Want me to help you find it?

The Loner

Ah, the ever-sexy lone wolf. Don't let his standoffish nature fool you—he's usually a man on the make even though nothing about his demeanor would otherwise suggest this. Loner Guys do very well with the ladies—particularly with ladies who have a bit of the loner in them themselves. They also get really popular girls who want to take a break from the crowd. They get girls who feel sorry for them, girls who want to support them, girls who are so enamored of the mythical "loner" image that they fall at the guy's feet. Only to later discover that guy they thought was a loner because he was so artistic, so talented, is really just a poser and at bottom a very lonely guy.

The Loner is very often a major operator. He's a version of the Smooth Talker but he's not talkative. Actually, the Loner usually says very little, and he gets a lot of mileage out of the rebel/artist/quiet type of image he puts on. He counts on women reading him as a guy with many deep and profound thoughts—thoughts they want to get him to share. While it's true that some loner guys are geniuses (and if you want to play the muse to this artiste, by all means go for it), do keep in mind that most of them are just ordinary guys who don't have a helluva lot to say. Basically, you can say anything to a Loner. No topic is really out of bounds. They can be approached with equanimity by Shy Girls, Comediennes, Helpers, Smooth Talkers, and Ditzes. Say whatever you wish to a Loner. But if he latches on to you because he doesn't want to be alone anymore, you'll just have to deal with it.

Just to break the ice, try these lines on your next Loner:

* "Are you standing here alone because you want to be alone?"
* "Don't tell me. They don't allow two people here at once?"
* "Excuse me, but could I borrow you for a few minutes? I need someone to watch my back."
* "What happened to your friend?"

Don't use these

The Taken Guy

He might be a Loner. He might be an Alpha. He might be Goofy. But no matter what his personality type, the fact remains—he's taken.

It can be a lot of fun to approach and flirt up a guy who isn't available. It's actually great practice and a way to have a little fun because the stakes aren't very high—after all, he's spoken for. So feel free to practice all your best lines and hone your skills on him. A great variation on the Taken Guy is the Very Married Guy. If they're in love with their wife and they've been married a long time, their wives are usually tolerant of their flirtatious behavior because they know that it's all talk and no action. On the other hand, some very married men are not really "taken," and if you start flirting with them, you could be opening a can of worms you didn't bargain for.

When you're approaching a Taken Guy, keep it fun and friendly—don't tread on territory that could get you into trouble. After all, you only want to practice your flirting a little bit, not cause a breakup. That said, try one of these lines to burn the memory of you into this Taken Man's mind:

* "I don't care if you're married."
* "So, tell me. How committed are you to your roommate?"
* "Was that your girlfriend getting on that bus? Gee, I bet you're going to be lonely this weekend."

Remember, everything you could say to a taken guy can either be harmless or harmful. It's not your exact words. It's your intention. If your intention is to have fun, anything you say, including openly sexual talk, goes. But if your intention is to wreak havoc, merely saying "hi" is provocative and potentially dangerous!

Confidence Is Key

WHAT'S THE MOST IMPORTANT THING TO HAVE WHEN APPROACHING A GUY FOR THE FIRST TIME?

a. **A great smile**
b. **Shiny hair**
c. **Fabulous shoes**
d. **Minty fresh breath**
e. **Confidence**

The answer, of course, is e. That's right, because if you have confidence, everything else will fall into place. However, if you've been hitting the garlic dip, you might want to pop an Altoid before making your approach.

A Little Ego Boost Never Hurt Anyone

By approaching a guy and talking to him, you're not only giving his ego a little bit of a boost, you're building your self-confidence as well. Your simple action of taking the initiative instantly accomplishes several things:

* It makes the guy feel attractive. (Men really are just like women in this regard. They love being made to feel attractive.)

* It says to him that he's been noticed by a female and that she's found him worthy.

* You're giving an assist to a shy guy. Most guys, actually, are pretty shy. When you take the initiative to talk to him

first, you're able to direct the conversation. You're in control! That shows confidence!

In short, by initiating conversation with him, you're sending him a clear and direct message that you're interested—and that's very flattering. Approaching a guy also tells him that you have confidence, *and absolutely nothing is as powerful an aphrodisiac as confidence.* Confidence is sexy. Confidence propels people forward, keeps their head up, keeps them looking straight ahead. Confidence is a life force. A woman can't move on in the world today without it. Think of a toddler girl just beginning to walk. For her to stand up and put one foot in front of another requires confidence that she won't fall down. And it's the same confidence that makes her take her first step, which leads her on to the next one. First she's taking a couple of baby steps. Then she's up on her own two feet and walking. Pretty soon she's got enough confidence that she's off and running. You've got to admire that!

But having the confidence to approach a guy isn't only good for *his* ego—it's great for yours, too. You're in control. You're having fun. You're calling the shots and controlling the conversation. You're seeing the positive results of cause and effect. You took action, and he responded in kind.

In a room crowded with other women, being the first girl to speak also gives you an edge over your competition. Don't believe me? Check out the story below.

If You Want It, Go for It, or Why a Woman Shouldn't Wait for a Man to Take Charge

Once upon a time a very long time ago there was a girl who wished more than anything that she could become a princess.

The likelihood of her attaining this coveted position on her own seemed, well, farfetched. For starters, her daddy wasn't rich. She wasn't an heiress. She didn't come from a royal family and she had no relatives, however distant, who were titled. Her wardrobe, while nice, was a bit meager and she didn't have the money to hire fine horses and a carriage. However, she did have one friend who was well placed (I think her friend was a publicist), who was able to secure her an invitation to a great ball. A prince, it was rumored, had promised to be there. The girl just knew that if she could only meet him and speak with him, he would be hers.

Luckily, she was able to borrow a ball gown that was just her size, and after she finished her shift moonlighting as a milk maid, the girl took her cows back into the barn and then soaked in a warm, refreshing bath and fussed a bit with her hair. She made sure to rub plenty of cold cream into her hands so her skin would be nice and soft when the prince held them. She caught a ride from a farmer who was headed into town to drop off a load of hay, taking care to make sure she was dropped off just far enough away from the ball so no one could see how she arrived. When she walked into the grand ballroom, she made sure to tell the footman, whom she knew to be a gossip, that something tragic and inconvenient had befallen her carriage but that he not mention it when he announced her. Of course, the footman told every man arriving about the lovely young woman stranded without her carriage and, before they even had removed their coats, a half dozen men were already prepared to offer safe ride home to the young lady they hadn't even met.

Inside the ballroom she recognized the prince right away. (She had seen his picture in a celebrity tabloid.) He was tall and dark and handsome, and she especially liked the way his dark brown eyes looked so sincere. So badly did she yearn to meet him that her heart pounded in her chest. Her only concern was that when she made her move to cross the room toward him, that her legs might be too weak to carry her.

The girl did have one teeny bit of a problem. She had no one to rely on to make an introduction, for she knew no one at the ball. She looked all around and saw there were at least a dozen beautifully coiffed young ladies wearing beautiful dresses, all peering coquettishly at the prince from behind their fans.

The girl took a sip of punch to quench her thirst, and the booze in the punch helped to restore her. She snuck a peek over to where the prince was standing and, lo and behold, he was looking right at her. He had noticed her! Feeling his eyes hot upon her, she once again brought the punch to her lips. As she took a long draught, she inclined her head slightly so that her eyes met those of the prince. Once she had his gaze, she gave him a quick smile and didn't look away.

The prince lifted his eyebrows in surprise.

Focusing her eyes directly on his face, the girl started toward him, walking in a slow, measured pace. He began walking, too, his stride matching hers. They came together dead center in the room in front of a hundred watching people. The girl curtsied to him the way she had imagined doing a thousand times before.

"Shall we dance?" she said, and the prince opened up his arms and she stepped into them. The orchestra leader immediately changed the tune and all eyes were drawn to the couple as they twirled about, a few of the other girls grimacing with displeasure when they saw they had been outdone. The ordinary girl had staged a coup. The music rose to a crescendo as the couple began a dance that would last their whole lifetime.

The moral of the story? A regular girl really can meet and woo a prince. All you have to do is talk to him!

So the next time you're out at a social function, don't be intimidated. Be resourceful! Sure, those other women at the party might have spent two hours on their makeup and outfits, but while they're all ganged up in the corner gossiping, you're the one actually talking to a guy.

How Aggressive Is Too Aggressive?

What's the difference between having confidence and showing aggression? Confidence is all about boldness and self-assurance. A little aggressiveness is good (it means you like to take the initiative) but a big display of aggression can mean that you're loaded for bear or carrying an ax.

Only you can gauge how aggressive you should be when approaching a guy. After all, there's always the risk of scaring him off. Much of the way you play it depends on your personal flirting style. It's really all a matter of attitude, timing and . . . delivery.

You may be wondering how far you want to take it—and that's entirely up to you. Just remember that even when you're coming on strong, sometimes less can be more. You can go for it without being too obvious. Remember, even neutral words can come off kind of gutsy if you are using them to advance on his turf.

Well, it's the same with what you say, as you can see by turning the page.

	Superbold	*Bold*
At the bar:	"Buy me a drink?"	"Your drink looks yummy. What is it?"
At a jazz club:	"Mind if I sit here?"	"Hmmm . . . I can't find an empty seat."
At the dog park:	"Your dog is so cute! Can I pet him?"	"I wish my dog was so well behaved. Maybe you can teach me your secrets?"
At the gym:	"Is that bench taken?"	"Have you tried the tanning beds?"

Are You an Interrogator or a Declarative Sentence Maker?

Basically almost any first thing or couple of things you'll say to a man fall into two distinct categories. You're either a Question Asker or a Statement Maker, depending on your natural flirtstyle. For example, Ditzy girls tend to be more of a Statement Maker, even if their statements are, well, ditzy! Interrogator girls naturally ask a lot of questions (it's how they're genetically wired), and Helper girls also tend to ask questions, although their questions are soft edged, not sharp and pointed. Small Talkers are ambidextrous. They can be Question Askers *and* Statement Makers—no problem! Comediennes find it easy to go either way, as long as what comes out of their mouth is funny. Shy Girls? They have to push themselves to say anything!

Asking a guy, any guy, a question is relatively easy. It's also pretty safe because the nature of questions is that they do require a response. So unless the guy is a bare-faced jerk with no manners whatsoever, if you ask him a simple question, he's gonna answer.

Here are some nice and easy questions that even the shyest lass can ask:

✳ "Can you tell me what time it is?"

✳ "How do I get to Washington Street?"

✳ "All that sneezing! Do you think that kid is contagious?"

To ratchet it up a bit, the questioning can get a bit bolder.

✳ "Would you mind very much if I asked you to refresh my drink?"

✳ "What do you think of girls who wear glasses? Should I take mine off?

A serious interrogator (i.e., a fearlessly nosy girl) might try one of these classic lines:

✳ "I was just wondering. Are you married?"

✳ "I see you're standing here all alone. Want to buy me a drink?"

Declarative sentences can also invite response. The statement, however, should be topic-based, something fairly obvious the guy can relate and respond to. Girls who are too timid to ask anyone a direct question often do very well taking the plunge by putting forth a well-rehearsed declarative statement. These lines work for timid girls but they can work for other girls, too. The wisdom of always having on hand a well-rehearsed all-purpose declarative statement is . . . it means you always have something to say! A few all-encompassing declarative statements you should always have in your arsenal are:

* "Boy, it's hot in here."
* "I'm thirsty."
* "I'm ready to party."

Every one of these lines has the added impact of sparking the man you're speaking them to into a state of arousal. The first line tells him you're hot. The second says you have a need for something wet, and the third says you're ready to boogie. Every one of these lines is a mild turn-on—which is their point!

Here are some other ways you can put declarative sentences into action:

* (At a club or event) *"It seems like they packed in a great crowd."*
* (At a concert) *"This music is awesome. I had no idea this band was so cool."*
* (On the third day at school in line at the cafeteria) *"The food is a lot better than I thought it would be. I just wish they could move the line along."*

Or, you can try one of these rather bold declarative statements based on your flirting type:

* Smooth Talker: *"I think you should just come with me."*
* Ditz: *"Oh! Pardon!"*
* Interrogator: *"It's really none of my business, but those look like Gucci loafers to me."*
* Shy Girl: *"I don't know what that means."*

* Helper: *"I think that could use a woman's touch."*
* Comedienne: *"Sure, ya do."*

TOO MUCH 'TUDE?

Five deep questions to ask yourself if your 'tude is coming on too strong:

* Do you get a secret thrill out of being the aggressor?
* Is your style becoming too barbed? Has anyone recently told you that you're mean?
* Have you always dreamed of being a "mean girl"?
* Is your favorite actress Angelina Jolie?
* Are guys walking away from you when you open your mouth?

If you've answered yes to two or more of those questions, watch yourself! It's one thing to be adorably quick and clever. It's another thing when you start alienating your target audience.

DO YOU KNOW HOW TO USE A GREAT OPENING LINE?

Take this teensy test to determine your "FQ"—your flirtspeak quotient!

1. **You're at a bar with your girlfriend. A cute pair of guys grab the stools next to you. The first thing to come out of your mouth is:**
   a. "How did you know we were saving those seats specially for a pair of cute guys like you?"

b. "We were just about to leave because there were no cute guys. But now that you're here . . . "

c. "I'm sorry, we were saving those seats for someone else."

2. You're at a party with your brother. He wants to introduce you to his hottie roommate. The first thing you say to the guy is:

a. "Funny. My brother never told me you were so [*insert compliment here*]." (You could use tall, or blond, or blue-eyed, or built, or any other positive physical attribute.)

b. "My brother has told me a lot about you."

c. "My brother loves your underwear."

3. You're at a wedding but you didn't bring a date. (Your mother told you lots of single guys would be there but, as usual, she was exaggerating). You walk up to the first decent-looking guy you can find who appears unattached. The first thing you say is:

a. "Isn't this a beautiful wedding?"

b. "Something tells me I'm never going to get married. It's just not my thing."

c. "I'm so afraid I'm going to die alone. I just want a husband!"

4. You're at a coffeehouse and the mood is mellow. You're with a small group of friends. A guy gets on the stage and recites an ostentatiously bad poem, but you like the look of him. When he gets off the stage, you:

a. Order a double espresso and send it to his table—along with a little poem you just scribbled on a napkin with your first name and cell phone number.
b. Invite him to join your little party.
c. Say, "You're not afraid of making a fool of yourself, are you?"

5. **You're at a function at work and you find yourself standing next to the boss. The *big* boss. This is your first opportunity to speak with him. You:**
   a. Tell him how much you love working for his company.
   b. Compliment him on his outstanding choice of tie.
   c. Ask him if the rumors about the takeover are true.

6. **You're stuck in a long line at the bank. The hunky guy in front of you is wearing one of those jumpsuits with his name embroidered over his heart. You can't resist saying:**
   a. I always wanted to wear an outfit that has my name on it.
   b. Is that really your name?
   c. Dudley? That's your real name? What was your mother thinking?

Scoring: Guess what? If you picked all a's, you're right on the money, honey! If you picked b's, you're close (but not close enough). If you picked c's, all hope is not lost, but you could use some brushing up on your skills before moving on to chapter 4.

Six Showstopper First-Impression Lines You'll Want to Put to Use Right Now

✳ "I never met a man I couldn't learn to love."

✳ "Is that a Ralph Lauren jacket? You look so good in it."

✳ "Your hair is awesome."

✳ "Your dog is adorable! He really suits you."

✳ "It's not often that I meet a guy with such good manners."

✳ "I thought it was time to leave but now that you're here, I think I'll just stay."

Six Things You Never Want to Say to a Man (unless your goal is to send him packing)

Men, you might have noticed, can be a bit squeamish. No matter how big and bad they are, or how brave and level-headed—especially when there's anything involving blood or crying or raving lunatics for example—certain words and phrases are guaranteed to send them running for the exits. Here are some prime examples of phrases better left unsaid when you're talking to (or even around) a man.

✳ "My period . . ."

✳ "Menopause . . ."

✳ "My ex-boyfriend always said . . ."

✳ "My ex-husband always said . . ."

✳ "I've got this sore . . ."

✳ "My father . . ."

Now that you've mastered breaking the ice, it's time to move on to chapter 4!

Chapter Four

Okay, I Said Something, He Said Something—Now What?

Get the Ball Rolling

Once you've crossed the River Jordan and have dazzled him with your brilliant opening line, how do you keep this guy's attention and promote his continued focus on you?

The answer, obviously, is to keep the ball rolling. In flirtspeak, this is most easily accomplished by keeping up a running stream of dialogue and/or questions that will provoke even the most recalcitrant guy into talking to you. Space those queries out, however. Don't batter him with a rapid-fire interrogation! The point is to keep the conversation flowing, not beat him over the head with so many questions that he thinks you're the Grand Inquisitor!

One Great Line Leads to Another

The importance of keeping the conversation going is that the two of you need to keep talking for a relationship to develop. It's only in the movies (or sexy chicklit novels) that two people who just met fall into bed or in love with each other based on a one-or two-sentence exchange. In real life, even the briefest of relationships must begin with dialogue. If you're working toward becoming a master flirter, think of it this way: If you don't keep on talking to him, how is he going to ask for your cell phone number?

If you are lucky enough to have come up with two outstanding lines you can deliver in a row, go for it. I call that the the one-two punch.

Here's an example of how a Smooth Talker might do it:

> She says: "I love that cologne that you're wearing."
> He says: "Really? Thanks."
> She says: "Did you pick it out yourself or was it your girlfriend?"

Mirror, Mirror

Another way you can keep a conversation moving after only a few truncated opening lines is to advance it by introducing a related topic. Example: You're at a loud, standing-room-only concert and an incredibly adorable guy is standing ten inches away from you. You catch his eye and use that moment to say, "This band rocks." Depending on what the guy says in response, which in all likelihood will be some slight variation of:

(a) "Yeah," (b) "You said it," (c) "This band sucks," (d) Inaudible grunt, your *advance* line should be:

    a. "Yeah, absolutely." This is mirroring, repeating what he said, but with an added word. Saying "absolutely" adds one more word to the total content, which is indisputably another building block in the development of communication.

    b. "I love metal! Metal tastes good!" This is another

variation of mirroring. You're reaffirming what he just said. But you're also telling him something about yourself. You've just given him information.

c. "What do you hate about it? Why do you think it sucks?" In many ways, this is the perfect exchange because the guy is giving you a response you can react to. Now you have a built-in conversation topic. You two could debate all night long which bands rock and which ones suck. Go for it!

d. There is no good response to an inaudible grunt. Grunters, and you may make a note of this, tend to be emotionally stingy, withholding guys who start manipulating you immediately by refusing to speak English. This guy is going to give you nothing to work with. He might not even want to talk to you. (Grunting is often guyspeak for "Go away.") Many extroverted, chatty women really go for this type of guy. Aside from the fact that usually Grunters are terminally good looking, one of their chief charms to some women is that the girls can do all the talking. Which is why if you find yourself starting to fall for a Grunter, just keep talking. Until the moment he stands up and walks away from you, as long as he keeps grunting, you've got him.

Talking About Something You Know Nothing About

Just because you brilliantly snagged his attention with your insightful comment about football (or car racing or fly fishing or whatever), doesn't mean you can rest on your laurels now. You've got to be prepared to hold up your end of the conversation if this subject continues. And that could be a problem!

Say you got invited/dragged along by a friend to one of those early fall afternoon "a day in the country" skeet shoots. A totally gorgeous guy you said hi to over by the cider and doughnuts just said hi back and suddenly you're talking skeet.

Worry not. You have a couple of choices here. You can prattle on for a few minutes, pretending you know what you're talking about, until you see an opening to change the subject. Or, you can come clean about your ignorance and further the conversation at the same time.

If you find yourself in foreign subject territory, don't panic! Use it to your advantage. This is a chance to get to know him a little better—and learn something new.

Sometimes admitting you don't know much on a topic is better than pretending you know a lot. So instead of pretending you're the All-State Womens' Skeet Champion, you can draw him out with any of these statements: What the heck is a skeet anyway?

* "How long have you been shooting skeet? Have you been doing it since you were a little boy?"
* "I wish I knew how to shoot. Maybe you could show me."

This tactic works for just about any situation. Take football, for instance:

* "You know, I was a cheerleader in high school but I never really understood this game."
* "That's so incredible! You were a college quarterback? Tell me right now. What was your most exciting moment?"
* "Who do you think will get to go to the playoffs? Who are you rooting for?"

Now let's try it with the Bookworm guy:

* ❋ "How do you like that novel? I've had such a hard time finding good fiction lately."
* ❋ "You're reading Shakespeare? I love *Measure for Measure*. It's one of the comedies. Know it?"
* ❋ "Loved that book *White Oleander*. Did you see the film?"

Can We Change the Subject?

Whether you don't know a lot about the topic at hand or you want to keep the conversation fresh and exciting, learning to change subjects gracefully is a wonderful tool to keep in your flirtation toolbox. There are tons of reasons why you might want to change the subject, including that the present topic has run out of steam. Ideally, what you don't want to do is change the subject abruptly. What you're looking for are natural segues. Think of changing the subject more as a conversational bridge to lead you from one topic to another.

Say, for example, you were talking about dogs, but you want to change the subject to *What is he doing this weekend?* Try this:

"Speaking of dogs, the main reason I don't have one is I go away a lot. Like this weekend, I'm going skiing. What are your plans?"

Say you notice his very cool boots. Try this:

"I love those boots you're wearing. Are they authentic Harley-Davidson? Hey, did you ever see *Easy Rider*?"

And from here, you can move on to making plans, like this:

"Well, if you loved *Easy Rider,* they're having a Dennis Hopper retrospective at ——— this weekend. Wanna go?"

Give Him the Spotlight

So you think he's cute, but you're nervous and blanking on what to talk about. When in doubt, talk about his favorite subject—him! What guy doesn't enjoy talking about himself? It's not really that all guys are hopelessly narcissistic (hahahaha) but truly, unless a guy is being grilled or is on the hot seat about something, he prefers to avoid discussing other men. The only thing a man will freely say about another man is something disparaging. Men can't help doing that, really. It's one of the laws of the jungle; men are hardwired to be competitive. When a woman mentions another man to a man, his instinct toward that man is to crush him. You can't fail to please a man if you ask him a personal question that allows him to (a) tell his life story, or (b) seize the opportunity to talk about himself in a way that casts himself in a good light.

Giving the guy the floor is a solid strategic position, conversation-wise. For one thing, you can relax. *He's* the one talking. Plus, you can learn a wealth of information about this guy from just listening to what he says. This may be the one and only time you'll ever hear about his family. If you start dating and getting serious, you'll want this info as ammo. If he tells a positive story about himself relating to work, friends, or somebody's child he saved, you've given him a chance to shine in your eyes. That in turn makes him feel good. If he's a decent kind of guy, next he'll ask you something about *you.* Congratulations if that happens. Well done! Now you're sharing your stories!

Starring: You

At certain points in the conversation you're going to want to turn the spotlight onto yourself. After all, you can't just talk about the guy all night! Besides, this is your chance to tell him something great about yourself. Here's some good things to share:

* A nice thing that happened to you that day
* A good deed you did
* The tough term paper you just finished (or job report if that's more applicable)
* That you're going home for Christmas

There are certain subjects you'll want to avoid, lest he get the Wrong Impression:

* This is the first morning in a week you didn't wake up with a hangover.
* There is nothing left in your bank account.
* Your sister just told you she's pregnant and she's unemployed and not married.

Manic Talker or Motormouth?

When you're talking to a guy, a friend, a co-worker, do you find yourself going on and on . . . and on and on . . . without taking a breath or allowing them to get a word in edgewise? If so, you might be a babbler. Need more empirical evidence? Let's start with this list:

You might be a babbler if . . .

* The only person who really listens to everything you say is your mother.

* Your therapist often looks sleepy. Very sleepy.

* If your last boyfriend said it to you once, he said it a dozen times: "You've told me that story already."

* In conversations online, people frequently say to you, "Your point?"

* Even your best friend has begged you to shut up.

While any good student of the flirtspeak method should have an arsenal of witty and interesting conversation topics on hand at all times, there *is* such a thing as talking too much. Talking excessively will not only prevent you from learning more about the guy, it may also turn him off.

ARE YOU A BABBLER?

Take this instant quiz to find out!

True or False? Everyone but your closest friends start edging for the door once you begin talking.

True or False? You have never, ever been at "a loss for words."

True or False? When you're on the phone with your guy friends, you hear toilets flushing in the background and the sound of microwave popcorn popping.

If you answered "True" to any one of those statements, face it: you're a babbler! But have no fear—by the time you're through with this chapter, you'll be armed with handy tips to keep babbling at bay.

The Nervous Babbler

Many babblers are nervous types who talk too much because they're . . . nervous. It's the opposite condition of being tongue-tied. Are you nervously babbling? Check off these telltale signs:

* You get interrupted but when you start to talk again, you forgot what you last said.
* The eyes of the man you are babbling to are starting to become glazed.
* Your tongue is tired.

The Needy Babbler

Other babblers are just needy. The only thing they can talk about is themselves. They can't help it, they are their only topic . . . which frankly gets pretty boring.

Signs that you're morphing into a Needy Babbler?

* You've talked about your roommate, your boss, your siblings, mother. His pupils are beginning to look fixed.
* You've said the word "I" nineteen times in ten minutes.
* You're whining.

The Happy Babbler

A third kind of babbler is the happy girl who hasn't noticed that she talks too much. She's not nervous. She's not needy. She's just a babble-mouth! She can change topics like nobody's business, hopping from cars to clothes to what's happening on her favorite reality show with blinding ease. Guys can be initially drawn to the happy babbler because she needs no prompting. She's usually in good spirits because she loves to talk. Beware, however, that even the cutest kind of babble-mouth can get on a guy's nerves. It's good to know when to shut up!

Hints that maybe you should just try being quiet:

∗   He has ceased to respond to anything you say.
∗   His eyes are rolling back in his head.
∗   He tells you to "stifle it."

Breaking Your Babbling Habit

The good thing about babbling is that it's easily fixed. Even the babbliest babbler can be reformed. Babbling, you understand, is just a habit, like a verbal tic. Again, most women babble because they're anxious and the sound of their own voice calms them down. This type of person is only relaxed when she's talking. You've experienced tons of women who feel exactly like this. They're the ones who are on their cell phone 24/7, talking and talking and talking.

Want to get a handle on your babbling habit? Check out these do's and don'ts:

Do speak in normal-length actual sentences that end in a period. So much of babbling is just sloppy run-on talking. When you say something, mentally provide yourself with proper punctuation.

Don't hop, skip, or jump from one subject to another. Stay on the topic.

Don't repeat anything you just said. A great many babblers say everything twice (because they think the first time they said it, no one was really listening).

Don't be afraid to let another person get a word in edgewise. The point of a conversation is that more than one person can speak.

Do break for pauses between sentences. These rests are your best cue to tell you that it's time to let your voice "take a rest."

Do give yourself a big pat on the back each time you let another person speak.

Okay, now you know what to do and not to do, but how can you put those things into action? Try any of these babbling Band- Aids:

Punctuation Situation. Speak in sentences that have endings. Banish the word "and" from between any sentence. Say, "After school I'm going shopping. Later I might catch a movie," not "After school I'm going shopping and I might stop by the video store and get a movie and maybe I'll see what everybody is doing later and should I call you?"

Talking Topics. Stick to one topic at a time. Don't cram a lot of subjects all together. For example, if you're talking about a party you're going to, don't also talk about what you have to pick up at the dry cleaner's (even if it is the outfit you're planning on wearing to the party).

Repeat Offender. Don't repeat the same information twice. It makes you sound like a parrot. (Plus it gives away the fact that you only said the thing twice because you thought nobody heard you the first time. That shows insecurity!)

Equal Exchange. You say something and then he says something. Don't hog the conversation. Let him get his chance!

Perfect Pauses. Take a breath between statements. Sometimes when we're babbling nervously, we forget to breathe.

Check the Laughter. If you're babbling and laughing simultaneously (duh, have you had too much to drink?) you're probably in danger of snorting. Guys sometimes say they find a snorting girl sexy, but mostly they find it to be really gross.

Congratulate Yourself. You've conquered your babbling habit if you've followed all the above tips!

How Much Talking Should You Do?

So when you're talking to a guy, exactly how much talking should you do? Research suggests that the average woman speaks three times as much as do men on a daily basis. So, the next time you're chatting up a guy, try to cut your chatter down by about a half and see what happens. If your guy is conversing with you in a moderate, measured manner, if he's not answering your questions immediately, if he seems like he's considering his words, take this as a *good* sign. It means that he wants to keep an ear on what he's saying while at the same time keeping an eye (and an ear) on you. When you encounter a guy like this, instead of rushing to fill the space with words, wait him out a little bit.

So if he waits two beats before responding to something you just said, when it's your turn to speak, wait four. If you're especially prone to gratuitous babbling, then this is a great way to slow yourself down—and keep his attention. Your pauses force him to listen so he can catch what you're saying. That's one way surefire way to get him hanging on your every word.

Group Speak

Whether you're a babbler or not, it's easier to keep the conversational ball rolling if you and the guy don't have to do all the work. That's why chatting up/beginning to flirt with a guy in a group situation is easier than when the two of you are alone. We covered some of this back in chapter 3 with the Flirtspeak 5, but now it's time to kick it up a notch and really put group speak to good use!

Remember that old adage about safety in numbers? Guys who are shy and awkward in a one-on-one situation with a girl automatically feel more secure when they're not alone. Surrounded by their buddies, they are more likely to open up their mouths.

On the other hand, bold guys are also easier for women (especially shy women) to handle when they're not alone. Girls who aren't brave enough to talk to a bold guy alone become more emboldened themselves when they're in a group where everyone is already relaxed and talking. Just knowing she's got a supportive group of friends around her helps a shy girl open up.

There are three steps you have to take to enter a "closed" group of people. You can think of it as kind of the ABCs of group speak:

Approach
Behavior
Control

Here's how you use the ABCs in a group situation:

Approach

You're at a party. So far you've been hanging in the kitchen with the booze and the food. The room is packed with chattering partygoers, but you can't find anyone who looks good to you, so you decide to scope out other rooms. A fun-looking group has taken over the den where they are excitedly talking and watching something on TV.

Here's where you use your approach. Step into the room (aka their space) and say:

"Mind if I join you? It's getting a bit rowdy out there."

Behavior

Sit yourself down. If there isn't an empty seat, create one. If no one immediately speaks to you, just wait awhile and listen. Get the gist of the conversation. As soon as someone says something you can contribute to, or there's a conversational lull, jump in but remember to stay on the topic! Your behavior is to fit in, not make any waves.

Control

Once you're in the boat, so to speak, sail ahead. The goal here is not for you to become the Queen of the Crowd although, if that happens, go to the head of the class! Your goal for control is simply to hold your own with the group. Once that's established . . . and this can happen within minutes, zero in on the guy you really want to talk to and begin directing half of your comments in his direction. Give him just enough direct eye contact to let him know you want to talk to him, but not so much that he feels like he's prey and you're a huntress. G-r-a-d-u-a-l-l-y devote yourself to talking to him and him alone . . . and then you're really cooking!

TIPS FOR TALKING IN GROUPS

✳ Don't hog the floor.

✳ Introduce topics that are of general interest to the group. For example, if you all just came from a movie, it's great to discuss the show.

✳ Don't be afraid to play the role of devil's advocate. What that means is that you're taking an opposing position to what the other person or persons are saying. A little conflict creates a new dynamic and keeps the conversation from running out of steam too quickly or going stale.

✳ Modulate your voice. Even if everybody else is shouting, keep yours from turning raucous. Remember, in a noisy situation, people always pay more attention to the person whose voice remains low.

✳ Make eye contact with everyone in the group, if you can. Don't intentionally ignore anyone . . . at least not completely!

✳ Avoid talking with your hands. Men find women who wave their hands to be unpleasantly distracting. Frankly, that kind of motion frightens them!

✳ Use other people's dialogue as a jumping-off point. For example, if someone tells a cute pet story, follow up with a cute (but brief) pet tale of your own.

✳ Make all stories brief but not so brief that you leave out the good parts!

✳ Stifle yourself if you find yourself growing argumentative. If there's a "button pusher" in the group, avoid responding to her/him.

What If the Guy You Want to Talk to Is Talking to Somebody Else?

Say the only guy you really find attractive in a group is already talking to another woman. Unless they're wearing matching wedding bands (and yes, you should check), you can still try to talk to him. The problem is, how do you maneuver the situation so that instead of talking to her, he'll be talking to you, short of shoving her out of the way?

Again, it all goes back to your ABCs. But in this situation, you've gotta be pretty subtle. You just have to use the group speak rules above. Sure, they may be a group of two, but unless they've got their arms wrapped around each other like a pair of mating snakes, he's fair game, honey, so go after him.

Here are a few ways to go about it:

Put her on Ignore

Walk right up to them and say, "Gosh, you guys look so cute together. Are you engaged or something?" If he says "No way," flash your sexiest smile at him. Put her on Ignore.

The big freeze

Approach him but immediately freeze her out. Without even acknowledging her presence, say to him, "Didn't we meet a few weeks ago? You look really familiar."

Plant yourself square in front of him (helps if you're wearing heels) and just introduce yourself. "Hi, I'm Jane. Now tell me, who are you?"

Befriend her

If he seems difficult to approach, you can always start by befriending her. Hey, it can't hurt, right? And who knows? You might just get a new girlfriend out of it. One way to do this is talk to her about the guy—right in front of him. You might say, "Don't you just love this guy's jacket? I wish I could find a jacket as soft as this." Then stroke his jacket. Voilà! You got in the first touch.

It's Two Against One—Now What?

Now let's focus on the guy. He's lovin' that he's got two women by his side. And any moment they might even break out into a fight over him! His reaction to this situation will either be to (a) try and play the two girls off each other, or (b) try and get both women to leave the party with him (based on the theory of "the more the merrier)."

He will do this by: (a) creating a conflict between the two women, or (b) setting up a scenario that brings them all closer together, like in a hot tub.

If he goes for choice (a), creating conflict, you must immediately align yourself on his side. What happens here is that you're contributing to the future ousting of this woman (chances are at this point she'll just give up and walk away). You can't feel bad about this. Your goal was to get rid of her anyway, right? When she excuses herself (why would she stand around when she's effectively been dismissed?), you have your chance to move in.

If he goes for choice (b), to set up a situation that brings you all closer, you have two choices of your own. You can either hang with it, or cut and run. It all depends whether you're into threesomes.

Play with Him

The best thing to do when you have to share a guy with another woman but you're absolutely not leaving the party, is simply to play with him. Tease him. Fool around with him. Be a bitch—a cute, sexy bitch! Loads of guys adore being slightly abused by a girly sadist! You can be a vixen torturing him, you can taunt him, you can cut loose with some of your more risqué stuff. You can be a bit smutty. You can say or do just about anything because . . . you're not alone. The other woman's presence automatically turns her into a kind of chaperone . . . and you can act up a storm because you've got an audience! So if you're feeling confident, give it a try. And he will remember you for the next time you meet, mark my word!

Another good thing to do when you're starting up a flirt with a guy who's talking to another woman is to not be like her. If you're too much alike, the guy won't be able to tell the difference.

So how do you indelibly imprint yourself into a guy's mind and make yourself stand out (and away from that girl!)? By deploying the flirt expert's secret weapon, the Art of the Verbal Tickle.

The Art of the Verbal Tickle

The verbal tickle is just what it sounds like. It's a tickle. Tickling teases. Tickling is playful and seemingly innocent, but it also sends an electrical charge along the tickled person's skin so, if used correctly, it can be very erotic. The great Eastern Indian book of love, the Kama Sutra, describes tickling as one of the great erotic acts.

A verbal tickle serves the same purpose as a physical tickle. Just as sexual current travels from one person to another during a physical tickle, the same kind of awesome physical charge happens when a woman says something that tickles the erotic fancy of a man.

A verbal tickle could be a double entendre—a phrase that can have two interpretations, one of them straight, the other risqué. It's a French term, and an invaluable one at that!

Some examples of the double entendre you can deploy with ease are:

* "Make mine a Sex on the Beach, please."
* "Where do you want me to put it?"
* "Hard day?"

The Dreaded Uncomfortable Pause

You've heard so many times about the dreaded uncomfortable pause. You've read about it in magazines, your girlfriends talk about it, it's a staple of every teen movie script.

The fact is, pauses in conversations are normal. People do stop and take a breath once in a while, and that's perfectly okay. Conversations do not usually follow a strict linear pattern. They wander. They wobble. They stop at a red light for a moment before moving forward. So the next time the object of your flirtation takes a pause, don't read too much into it. He could be catching his breath. He could be thinking about what to say next—like considering a chess move. He might even be working up the courage to ask you out!

So before you label every lull in a conversation "uncomfortable," think about that. The majority of lulls are nothing to be feared.

Genuine uncomfortable pauses can happen when something discomforting happens during the conversation. Maybe one of you said something that sent up a red flag to the other person. Maybe the two of you were gabbing right along, talking about celebrities. Out of the blue he announces he despises women who get plastic surgery, when you've just been considering it. You instantly figure you're going nowhere with this guy and that's what the pause is about. But wait a minute. Maybe the pause is just to give you a chance to regroup, to collect your thoughts. You can even seize the moment during the uncomfortable pause to challenge him. Keep the conversational ball rolling by saying, "Why, you look like a guy who just loves big boobs. If they look good and feel good, do you really care if they're real or not?"

Why Do Uncomfortable Pauses Happen?

There are so many reasons for uncomfortable pauses, it's difficult to count them all. The most common reasons why they happen are:

* You were going along great but then his date just walked back into the room. Oops, did she just catch you two flirting?
* He just remembered that he's married.
* He was pretending to understand what it is you do for a living but then the ceiling of his comprehension was reached.
* You just realized that you're no longer attracted to him and you're busy processing that thought.
* His cell phone rang and he decided to take the call. Right there.
* Both of you at the same moment decided you really don't have anything new to say to each other.

* The very best reason for an uncomfortable pause is that you both suddenly realized that you "have chemistry" and now you're wondering what's going to happen next.

A couple of things can happen in the wake of an uncomfortable pause:

* You find a way to get past it and keep the conversation going.
* You realize that you're mutually not that into each other and it's time to end the conversation.

Pause or Fast Forward?

A meaningful way to look at the uncomfortable pause is to view it as a tool to determine what is really going on between the two of you. Is this flirt going anywhere—or has it reached a dead end?

If you're really into him and you want to keep things going, why not try allowing the pause to give you both a chance to be quiet and simply look into each other's eyes? If the mutual attraction is there, you'll both feel it.

Here are some signals that he's into you to help you along:

* You found yourselves staring into each other's eyes.
* Suddenly, even though you were just chattering your heads off, now you're both tongue-tied.
* Things were going along supersmoothly until he asked you a question that made you blush. It's going to take a moment for you to recover . . . hence the pause!

If you're not that into him, you can even verbally address this head on by saying something like, "Well, we seem to have run out of time here, so, um, like, talk to you later?" which hurts no one's feelings and leaves you a way out.

SIX TIPS FOR EVADING THE UNCOMFORTABLE PAUSE

There are some things you can do to detour having an uncomfortable pause before it even happens. Here's some common conversational pitfalls you'll want to avoid like the plague:

Do neatly sidestep certain dangerous topics that can only leave the object of your flirtation with . . . nothing good to say. Bringing up your ex-boyfriend, your present boyfriend, the number of times you've been engaged, your credit card debt, your recent descent into madness that required a week of hospitalization, how much your feet hurt . . . these are all conversation stoppers with a capital CS.

Don't try to babble over a few moments of silence. Yes, your words will cover up the silence, but since they're just noise, it might be doing more harm than good.

Do think ahead to topics that will advance the present conversation even as it seemingly swims along. You don't want to be caught off guard when the subject runs its course.

Don't hesitate to throw in a joke or a funny line you heard/stole from a movie or somebody else. Humor is a great tool to use to foil conversational ennui.

Do take charge of the emotional context of the communication if you see it's headed down a grim path. For example, say you're talking about your pet with a guy when he suddenly offers that he just had to give his pet up. Unless you're a Helper girl and you want to use this information as a segue to turn on your comforting high beams, sad news subjects should be cut off at the pass. Ninety-nine percent of most uncomfortable pauses are caused by major bummers.

Once they get rolling, Uncomfortable Pauses can be overcome. Consider these scenario alternatives to get the conversation rolling again.

Sample Scenarios for Overcoming the Uncomfortable Pause

The *He's a Snob* Scenario

He says: "What kind of films do you like?"

She says: "I love romantic comedies."

He says: "I said 'film.' In my book, romantic comedies are movies, not films."

Uncomfortable pause: She doesn't know what to say next because she feels put down.

The save

She says (diluting his snobby comment): "So you say! I didn't realize there was such a big difference!" (Now they can go on to debate the difference between "movies" and "films.")

The *Oops, Did I Just Put My Foot in My Mouth?* Scenario

She says: "I just came back from this incredible vacation. I was at a resort in Ojai. Have you ever been to that part of California? It's gorgeous."

He says: "No, but what's the name of the resort? My sister went to one there a couple of months ago."

She says the name of the spa.

He says: "Isn't that a fat farm? My sister's pretty fat."

Uncomfortable pause: Uh-oh. Now she's crossed the TMI line—Too Much Information.

The save

She says: "Yeah, it is a fat farm, tee-hee. I just lost fifteen pounds off my butt. Take a look. Whaddya think?"

The *We're Coming from Two Different Universes* Scenario

He says: "Newport is fantastic. My family always summered there. How do you know Newport?"

She says: "I was a waitress there last summer."

Uncomfortable pause: They're both silent while considering the ramifications of this exchange. He'll never bring her home to meet Mother and she knows it.

The save

She says: "Ever mess around with a townie?"

How to Make the Uncomfortable Pause Work for Instead of Against You

You may discover during an uncomfortable pause that the discomfort is being caused by an abundance of physical chemistry between you. You both stopped talking because you're getting hot over each other! You'll know this is happening if your bodies are beginning to talk. Maybe you're leaning toward him, and his eyes haven't left your lips. Maybe he's playfully touching your arm and you're tossing your hair. Throw in a little dry mouth and what you've got is an uncomfortable pause caused by a chemical attraction!

If real life was more like the movies, the two of you would pause, make eye contract, then begin a hot make out session—no need for further dialogue necessary!

But alas, real life is nothing like the movies, so when you're confronted with a living, breathing uncomfortable pause, you need real ways to get past it. The best thing to do if you experience this kind of uncomfortable pause is take a moment. Savor it. You don't have to act on what is happening at all right now. Just breathe it in, inhale it. Just like the famed "hesitation step" a bride is instructed to take down the aisle on her way to the wedding altar (she's meant to slow down so she doesn't look like a wanton hussy desperate to leap into her man's arms), the uncomfortable pause serves the purpose of slowing down a girl who just met a guy she's powerfully attracted to. Magic has passed between you. It could be the hard thump of sexual desire or one of those romantic lightning bolts that says you may have just found your soul mate. Whatever it is, use the pause as your chance to clearheadedly consider how you want the next phase of your communication to grow.

Turn Something Embarrassing into Something Funny

Awful things do happen that result in a dreadful pause. Those are the pauses that heavily rest in the air between you like the smell of skunk, or a fart. Actually those things can be funny. If it's skunk you suddenly smell, both of you can yell "Ugh!"

Say you're with a guy and you're laughing so hard that your butt does give off a little poot. This happens lots of times when you're laughing. Don't pretend it didn't happen even if you wish the floor would just open up and swallow you just like that. You farted? Just go on and laugh about it! A little poot between two people who don't really know each other is just like a whoopee cushion. React to it like it is and you'll be less freaked out!

There *are* ways to save the day and bail you out of an embarrassing moment so you're not stuck standing there in the dry desert of an uncomfortable pause. Try one of these quick-fix lines:

Situation: He just dripped hoisin sauce down the front of your new blouse.
You say: "Ya know, these darn caterers. Can't they ever do hors d'oeuvres that aren't drippy?"

Situation: You assured him your purse pup is completely housebroken but Binky just tinkled on his rug.
You say: "Gosh, where do you keep the paper towels? Let me clean that up!"

Situation: You invited him over to your apartment but when you rummage in your bag, you can't find your keys. There's a

long uncomfortable pause as he considers whether to wait while you call a locksmith (which might mean hanging around in your hallway half of the night) or bail on you or what.
You say: "Hey, I'm not going to worry about this right now. Let's shoot on over to your place."

Situation: You just realized the back of your pants are ripped.
You say: "Gee, I knew these pants were on their last legs. Let's duck into a store right now so I can do some emergency shopping."

Situation: You're having an intensely flirtatious personal exchange with the new guy in a coffee bar when your old boyfriend walks in and shoots you a withering glare. The new guy notices and comments.
You say: That guy who was just shooting daggers at me with his eyes? Don't know him.

Lemme Hear Your Body Talk

If you're looking for other ways to keep the conversation ball rolling, there's nothing like body language to heat things up a little bit!

Body language is a way of talking to someone without talking. It's a system of eye and body movements that act in place of words. Sometimes the language is inadvertent, even unconscious. For example, when someone asks you a question and you start blinking, you're telling your questioner that you're either nervous or lying. If you cross and uncross your legs a few times in front of a guy, you're telling him you find him attractive. The language can be deliberate, too. If you suck on an ice cube in front of the bartender, he knows you're considering going home with him.

Body language is a useful tool to have in your flirtspeak arsenal, whether you drop yourself in his lap (shocking but potentially delicious) or just rest your hand ever so briefly on his arm. A lot of girls are naturally touchy-feely. They're always throwing their arms around someone or they kiss everybody, sometimes on the lips. Or the touch is more . . . sympathetic, consoling. The Helper personality does this very well. Just remember though that, when you're dealing with strangers, touching men can be risky.

But you don't have to actually touch a man to tempt him with body language. Sometimes it's just a look you give him.

Enticing Eyes

Eyes are always the most important tool to use when you've just met the guy. Use your eyes to telegraph a message. Your strong gaze tells him you're expressing strong interest. An arched eyebrow can be used either to indicate surprise (as in "You're kidding!") or adorable skepticism (as in "Are you for real?"). Closing your eyes for a moment can be very intriguing. He'll ask you if you're sleepy (your cue to say something cute), or he'll wonder if he's losing your interest, which will make him put some effort into getting it back. This is a smooth move because it forces him to do some work!

It's also true that the eyes are the mirror to the soul, so pay attention to his. If they're focused on you, that's a green light! If his eyes lock on yours, he's either informing you that he really wants to get to know you better—or he's a very accomplished flirt. If his eyes are wandering in the middle of your conversation, you're probably losing him. Make one more attempt to regain his interest, but should that fail, politely move on. He's just not the guy for you.

Don't Touch Him!

If you want to deliver a walloping body comment without laying a finger on him, what you want to do is angle your bod a bit in his direction to give him a better view. Or put one finger to your lips in the classic pose of intense listening, but which also can mean, "Shhh, let's whisper." This gesture draws his eyes to your lips.

That said, any location on your body where you put your own fingers works as a pointer to that body part. If you cross your arms so that your hands are wrapping around your own shoulders, the man will look first at your hands and then at your shoulders. Are those shoulders smooth and naked? He'll find that soooo sexy!

Definitely make sure your hands are always attractive looking and smooth to the touch. You don't have to invest in professional manicures—although they sure are nice. Just keep your nails clean and shapely, slather on some of your fave moisturizer (preferably in a yummy scent), and you're good to go!

POLISH PERFECT—WHAT YOUR COLOR SAYS ABOUT YOU

* Red nails signal you're a red hot mama. Red nails also read "tough."
* Pale pink nails say you're shy.
* Black nails scream "Goth!"
* Purple nails say you're a party girl who favors late-night clubs.

* Blue nails say you're either a Ditz or a young fashionista. Did you just tell him you're a clothes designer?
* Earth-tone nails imply that you're kind of earthy (or just mean you wear a lot of brown).
* Fuchsia nails shout Southern Princess. Do you hail from the Deep South or are you just channeling your inner Reese Witherspoon?

Body Language or Booty Language? What's the Difference?

Booty language is a little different from regular body language in that it's more direct, more pointed. Booty language is unmistakably about sex. The message is deliberately provocative. Booty language is a way of saying check out the goods—without ever having to utter the actual words, "Check out the goods."

So if you've got it and you want to flaunt it, stick out your chest. Show some leg. Cock your hip. Bend over!

BODY LANGUAGE TIPS FOR WHEN YOU FIRST MEET HIM

* Stand close. Sit closer.
* Engage in brief but intense eye contact.
* Point your foot at him if the seating arrangement allows it.
* Keep your body language fairly ladylike. In other words, don't climb in his lap or shove your boobs in his face unless you want to be taken for a very aggressive woman.

If you feel yourself freakin' because it's going soooo well, excuse yourself briefly and walk away. Take a moment to clear your head and get your heart to quit pounding. At this point you don't want to blow everything by letting the guy know how much you like him!

Part Two

closing the Deal

Chapter Five

Working It

You've come a long way, baby! When you first picked up this book, your metaphorical bag of handy pickup lines was practically empty. Your cupboard of sassy comments was bare. Back then, you didn't know a thing about talking to guys and now you're halfway down the road to becoming an expert! At this point in the game you know what kind of flirt you are (the kind that comes naturally . . . sort of like your natural hair color . . . or not!).

Whether you're a Comedienne or a Shy Girl or you've got a bit of a Ditzy side, you now are equipped with the added armament of body language and you have your killer opening lines at the ready. Most of all, you now comprehend the importance of being able to make flirtatious conversation.

Another thing you've picked up along the way is a better feel for which men are worth talking to and which ones you should run away from. You've learned volumes about volume control (when to shout and when to whisper), and talking in groups no longer scares you. All your hard work and taking of those baby steps have paid off to create a foundation that you can stand tall and flirt on. It's time to take your act out on the road, girl, and drive it!

Let's go!

Sexy Subtext

As you have now learned, a girl can talk to a guy just about anywhere. Men are all around if you only open your eyes to see them. Look around! The world is full of men, and girls who whine there are no cute guys are not really looking!

The bad news is, there's no surefire way to tell when, where, or how you'll meet a guy. What matters is knowing what to say when you *do* finally meet him! So remember, there's a fun flirtation around every corner—you just have to keep your eyes open and make the most of every situation you're in—and back it up with sexy subtext.

Wherever you do go to find your guy, remember it's not so much what you say as how you say it. We're not just talking pointed remarks or sultry whispering here, although if you've mastered those, go to the head of the class!

What's at work here is subtext, or the story within the story. Sure, you can ask a guy what time it is, but if you really want to grab his attention, he has to get it that you're opening the door to sharing a flirt with him. That flirt could last five seconds or five hours . . . it doesn't matter how long the thing lasts, only that it happened.

The story within the story could be about anything. The cover story, the one that's out in the open, just has to be in context with the situation.

Imagine this scenario. It is 12:45 A.M. and you're just coming home from a concert. You're at the Greyhound bus terminal waiting for the last bus to start loading. There are a lot of people milling around, and you can tell it's going to be a crowded ride. You spy a cute guy loitering around who seems to be waiting for the same bus. You hope like hell you can sit next to the guy and maybe spend the ride talking to him. After all, you're going to have to sit next to somebody for two and a half hours. Shouldn't it be him?

The most obvious story here is the one you tell yourself. Your story is you want to sit next to this guy because:

* He's cute and doesn't look like a madman even if he does have a pierced ear and a tattoo of an Incan demon on his ankle.
* At this hour all the other possible seatmates are downright creepy or smelly.

How do you convey this to him and make it happen?
You approach him and say:

* "Didn't I just see you at the concert?"
* "How's your coffee? Mine tastes awful."

If, once you've initiated the conversation, things are going well, you can say, "Would you mind sitting next to me on the bus? You seem perfectly normal and, frankly, these other people are scarin' me." The damsel-in-distress card is a great one to play in a scenario like this. Guys love to be the knight in shining armor.

Those are your *actual words*. But the *subtext* of those words is: You think he's cute and friendly enough that you *want* to sit next to him.

Just a word of warning: No matter how subtle your subtext, chances are that the object of your flirtation will think you desire him. This is not necessarily a bad thing. It's just that the male mind is programmed to think that 99 percent of anything a woman says to a man that doesn't fall into the category of outright criticism means "She wants me."

Hard as it is to believe, in a man's mind every conversation with a woman is actually something like this:

She says: "Gosh, it's so late. I hope I don't fall asleep and miss my stop."
He hears: *She's wants me.*

She says: "Will you wake me up before I get to my stop? "
He hears: *She's inviting me over to her place.*

Because you now know how guys' minds work, stay alert to sending him signals that your interest is sexual. In other words, once you're sitting beside him on that bus, maintain some physical distance, even if it's millimeters. Don't brush your hand against his. Don't knock knees. Your faces can get close together once you're talking, but don't lick your lips. Don't talk about your body (which overly draws attention to it), or share with him any misbehavin' you did at the concert. (If you tell him you've had a lot to drink, you shouldn't get mad if he tries to take advantage.) And resting your tired head on his shoulder is absolutely out!

Now let's try out some other locations beyond the Greyhound terminal.

At the beach

The man you have your eye on is building a sandcastle.

Your line: "I've always had a thing for turrets."
The subtext: Come up to my place, baby, and play Lancelot to my Guinevere.

At a large discount appliance shop

The man you have your eye on is eyeballing refrigerators.

Your line: "I'm trying to decide on one of these, too. What do you think is better? Freezer on top or freezer on bottom? Or do you think I should just go for the side by side?"

The subtext: Who gives a damn about freezers? It's the hot spots I'm interested in. Let's get side by side and snuggle.

At your apartment

The man you have your eye on is the service guy out on a repair call.

Your line: "I know by day you're just the cable guy, but I bet at night you're a rock and roll god."

The subtext: Show me what you're wearing under that silly jumpsuit.

At a small, mostly empty restaurant near closing time

The man you have your eye on is your waiter whose been doing a lot of unnecessary hovering.

Your line: "Could you ask them to lower the lights?"

The subtext: Close the joint now and let's go someplace and grab a drink.

At a retro dance club

The man you have your eye on is already on the dance floor

Your line: "Do the hustle?"

The subtext: Dance with me!

During happy hour

The man you have your eye on is jockeying for position in front of the barbecued wings platter.

Your line: "I'm starving ."
The subtext: I'm starved. I'd like to eat you up.

Match Game

If you still want a little extra practice, here's a fun thing to do. It's called Match The Line to the Location/Situation. You provide the pencil!

The Location	*The Line*
In line at a coffee bar	"Now here's something I really need."
At the bus stop	"What do you think? Are diamonds a girl's best friend?
In the veterinarian's waiting room	"You look about my size."
In the stacks at the library	"Snow me?"
At a costume party	"Going up?"
Waiting for the elevator	"Don't you wish you had wheels?"
At a tag sale	"Read anything good lately?"
In line at the ski lift	"Let's not fight over these lattès."
Outside a dressing room	"Let me guess. You're Quasi-modo."
By the jewelry counter	"Have you had all your shots?"

Harmless Flirting vs. Flirting Like You Mean It

It takes two to tango and at least two people to flirt. There are two types of flirting:

1. **Harmless flirting—This is flirting to pass the time of day.**

2. **Flirting like you mean it—This is more goal oriented, the goal being that this guy might want to go out with you and you want to go out with him.**

Depending on your situation, you can employ either of these tactics just about anywhere you go.

Harmless Flirting

Harmless Flirting makes ordinary life more entertaining. Try these Harmless Flirts on for size . . . but learn to recognize the Stop signs.

Situation: You're in the doctor's office and the doc is really cute. Like, disarmingly cute.

You say: "I was looking at your diplomas and I see you went to Tulane. I bet you just loved Mardi Gras."

If he says: "For a couple of years there I thought a hurricane was just the name of a drink"—he's flirting!

If he says: "I wouldn't know. I never went to it"—he's a stick. He's not open to harmless flirting. Stop right away!

Situation: You're seated next to a cute guy at a fund-raiser. The dress code is dress up. You catch him sneaking a peek at your cleavage.

You say: "In case you were wondering, they're real."

If he says: "I'm impressed"—he's flirting! Carry on!

If he says: "I don't know what you're talking about"—he is so not a flirt and is annoyed he got caught. Move on!

Situation: You're looking at sound systems for your wheels. The salesman is mighty attractive.

You say: "I'm looking for a system with a great bass. I'm really into classic rock."

If he says: "Oh, a Guns n' Roses girl, are you?"—he's up for a little flirting!

If he says: "What is your price range? Let me show you what we have over here"—he's not.

Flirting Like You Mean It: You Make the First Move

There will be times when your flirting has a purpose—like you want him to ask you out. Try these lines when your intentions are serious.

Girl: *"I bought this perfume specifically because I heard it really turns men on."*

Guy: *"It's working."*

Girl: *"Why don't you come closer to get a better sniff?"*

Girl: *"I read somewhere that guys are either leg men or breast men. Which kind of guy are you?"*

Guy: *"I like what you've got."*

Girl: *"Sweet. But come on. Which do you really prefer?"*

Flirting When You Mean It: He Makes the First Move

Use these not at all subtle lines when you really mean business—Flirty business!

Guy: *"I love it when a woman wears her hair up like that."*
Girl: *"Yeah, it makes it easier for the guy to kiss her neck."*

Guy: *"How many times are you going to keep doing that?"*
Girl: *"My motto is just keep trying until you get it right."*

A Quick Word About E-Flirting

Sometimes you'll be online, flirting your head off, when you realize you don't have a clue who you are talking to. The screen name isn't giving anything away; honestly, does a name like "Poewhit" mean a man or a woman? Before you get in too deep and start falling for someone whose gender isn't really your thing, take a moment to toss out these pithy questions:

* ✳ "So what are you anyway? A man . . . or a woman?"
* ✳ "Who am I talking to exactly?"
* ✳ "Just tell me now. Do you have hair on your legs or what?"
* ✳ "You say you have a thing for high heels. Is that wearing, 'em or just admiring 'em?"
* ✳ "PMS. You know what that is, right?"

Who's Holding the Flirtstick?

Just because you're putting yourself out there and flirting like a pro doesn't mean that you're guaranteed a level playing field. There's always going to be someone holding the flirtstick—and it's not always going to be you. This section will help you guard against being outflirted at your own game—or using it to your advantage.

The Control Flirt

Despite even your most charming efforts, you're eventually going to run into a guy who is seemingly impervious to your flirtatious ways. No matter what tactic you try, nothing sticks! But a seasoned flirtress is never easily discouraged! If you come across a guy who immediately throws up a wall to your attempts, try a little reverse flirting psychology on him. Rather than turning up the playfulness, pull a total turnaround and become blatantly nonflirtatious—aka the Strictly Business approach. Make it clear that the furthest thing from your mind is stirring up even the tiniest whiff of a flirtatious atmosphere. Express that message by maintaining utter control of your words, your tone of voice, and your body language. Basically that means no laughing, no teasing, no hair tossing, no smiling. If you employ the Strictly Business tactic, 99 percent of the time the man you are now deliberately *not* flirting with will now try to flirt with *you*.

A great tactic to use here is make sure he gets your business card. At the last moment, scribble your personal cell number on it, adding, "Sometimes this is the best way to catch me."

Looking for more ways to flirt covertly? Try these moves on for size:

* Invite him to a business lunch.
* Invite him to discuss some business over a game of squash or golf (make sure you know how to play before you use this ruse).
* Tone of voice is everything. If you say, "Here's my number" straightforwardly, as if you're leaving it for the plumber, he won't know if you're flirting with him or not. That's intriguing!

These lines leave the door open to further communication that may later turn . . . flirtatious!

The lesson here is that some men have to be the person who flirts first—they're not control freaks—they're control *flirts*. It's a control thing. They have to make the approach. With some men, if you behave like you're in the least bit interested, they'll turn on the Teflon and pretty soon you'll be out of luck.

However, if you like a bit of a challenge, give Mr. Teflon a try. But beware—his need for control might extend to far more than flirtatious conversation, and the last thing you need is a guy who's trying to control every aspect of your life!

The Natural-Born Flirt

It should come as no surprise that there are men out there who are much flirtier than you. Some of them were just born flirty—usually these guys were adorable infants and toddlers who learned the art of flirting in the cradle. How? Because so many adult women, beginning with their own mothers, have always flirted with them! Babies learn early that when they smile, some woman always smiles back! They quickly put two and two together, the cause-and-effect thing that when they make their facial expressions beguiling and charming, they can charm the pants off anyone. Cooing and giggling elicits more cooing and giggling. At the baby stage, all this gained knowledge is subconscious.

Animals, of course, flirt with one another (and with their caregiving humans) all the time. It's nature's way of ensuring that those who need to be taken care of get taken care of! On the most instinctive level, flirting is a mode of survival as well as a form of communication.

Traits of the Male-Natural Born Flirt

∗   Handsome
∗   Either very sparkly-eyed or has that low-lidded sleepy look . . . either way, his eyes are a main asset
∗   Knows how to talk to women . . . all women
∗   Good with babies and young children
∗   Never at a loss for words

Is He Outflirting You? A Checklist

∗   His smile is so dazzling and disarming that you forget what you just said.
∗   His mouth is moving, but what's the message?
∗   Is it a hallucination or is half of what he's saying a double entendre ?
∗   You can't tell if he's teasing.
∗   You're experiencing a loss of control. Are you being beaten at your own game?

You always know the moment when you've been outflirted. Sure, you're the one who made the approach, but now he's the one holding the flirtstick. He's in control now, since he's literally flirting rings around you! The questions you want to ask yourself here are, (a) do you want that big bad flirtstick back, or (b) Are you willing to share it?

When Two Big Flirts Get Together . . . Is It Fireworks or What?

How can you tell if you'll be one of those amazing couples who flirt together happily ever after . . . or do you worry if your combined and terribly potent flirt energies will blow the fire out?

Take this test to learn more.

1. *True or False?* **You love that you're steppin' on each other's lines, completing each other's sentences.**

2. *True or False?* **You wish he'd be quiet for a minute so you could get some good lines in.**

3. *True or False?* **You're thrilled to meet somebody who's just as flirtatious as you.**

4. *True or False?* **You don't mind sharing the lime-light.**

5. *True or False?* **You think it's cute that he's borrowed all your great lines.**

Answers:

1. **True: You and this guy are going to get along fine.**
   False: Look out! You're not the type of gal who enjoys this kind of competition!

2. **True: You're probably going to get tired of this guy fast.**
   False: It sounds like you've found your match!

3. **True: If this relationship definitely has a chance.**
   False: Sounds like you like 'em a bit more on the shy

side. Maybe you should continue in your search for the ultimate flirtation.

4. True: You don't mind sharing the limelight? Isn't that generous?

False: You mind very much having your brilliance mirrored by an equal flirtspeak expert? Hmm, move on, honey. There's too much room here for conflict!

5. True. Is it possible you've found your ideal mate?

False. Omigod, you've taken up with a thief! He's stolen all your best material and appropriated it for himself!

When it turns out that you have met your flirt match and it doesn't look like it's going to be a match made in heaven, i.e., romantic, you can make lemonade out of lemons. Capitalize on the situation. Combine forces and create a flirt team of two and work a room together. You haven't made an enemy. Instead you've found your wingman.

Outflirted by Another Woman? How to Make the Best of It

The same way you can be outsmarted by another woman, you can also be outflirted. This happens when two women are simultaneously flirting with the same man . . . an all-too-common bar/party situation. Oftentimes, there is only one really decent flirt prospect and unfortunately some woman is already wrapping a noose around him. While the old you would have immediately talked herself out of going over and approaching him, the new you is going to dive right in and commence flirting! At this point, you're not going to take a backseat to anyone!

In your attempts to outflirt another woman, you may have to un-learn some of the previous lessons you've been taught about breaking into group conversations.

When you make your approach, begin by virtually ignoring him and concentrating your flirtatious skills on her instead. Com-pliment something she's wearing or say you like her hair. If you get her talking about herself, it prevents her from further engaging him. As you work the conversation, take note of the guy's bore-dom/enthusiasm factor. If he's hungrily hanging on her every word, gradually extricate yourself from the scene. To put it bluntly, you struck out. But if he seems even the tiniest bit bored or his eyes are roaming around the room seeking the fastest escape route— now's the time to make your move. The next time there's a break in the conversation, ask the guy something about himself. Just change the subject to something that involves him, and in no time at all, he'll be eating out of your hand.

What If She Won't Take the Bait?

Occasionally you'll run into a girl who is truly a flirtworthy op-ponent. She won't fall for your ploy of trying to turn the tables on her. Not only does she adroitly manage to find ways to show off her cleverness, but she knows how to keep working the guy into the picture, too. Is she succeeding? Is he smiling at her more than he's smiling at you? Is he still giving her the lion's share of his at-tention? Is he excusing himself and bidding you a farewell even as he's saying to the other woman, "Let's go?" If he actually leaves the party with her . . . well, you've been outflirted. You lose!

On the other hand, if he's not going anywhere and he seems interested in talking to both of you, that means you're still in the game. So keep playing! If you can, use her the way you would a wingman to keep the conversation flowing and to keep up that aura of energy that comes when people are drawn to/amused/ excited by each other. Eventually he will choose one of you over the other to focus his attention on. But until that moment happens, just keep flirting!

Omigod, He's Interested!

You've worked really hard to get his attention and now you've got it! Maybe you've successfully outflirted another woman. Maybe you've employed all of your favorite flirtspeak tools and you've got the flirtstick firmly in your grasp. However you go here, it's a real achievement (let's face it, the competition out there is fierce), but it *does* present a dilemma. How interested is he? And how can you tell?

* *He offers to get you another drink.* This means he wants to keep talking to you. It also means he is hoping you'll get drunk enough to make out with him out in the parking lot.

* *He says he has to split but asks for your cell number.* This means he has another rendezvous at that moment but he might call you later if that doesn't work out.

* *He says he has no other plans for the evening and do you want to hang out.* He's clearly into you and putting it out there.

✱ *He acts like he really likes you but keeps mentioning some other woman.* This means he's seeing someone but if she dumps him, you're next in line.

✱ *He acts like he really likes you but mentions he lives far away.* This means he's feeling you out about how you feel about one night stands or possible long distance relationships.

✱ *He's very smooth and flirtatious.* This means he's used to getting women to fall for him. You're nothing special . . . yet.

THE 3-HOUR RULE

Even when things are going good, put a three-hour limit on your first meeting/date. Why?

✱ If real chemistry has kicked in, cutting it off after three hours leaves him wanting more.

✱ You don't have enough time to tell him so much that you either frighten or bore him.

✱ It's not enough time to get too physical—no matter what.

✱ And if you didn't like him all that much, three hours is already too much of an effort for you to have put in. Move on!

Oops, Did I Just Cross a Line?

Even if you're the smoothest flirt, you may occasionally blurt out something you wish you hadn't. It might just be a little thing . . . something you thought was funny but he took as an insult, or maybe your quip about something about his appearance or his car or his dog or his living situation made him uptight. Okay, damage done! Now how do you fix it? You can choose different answers based on your flirting style.

Any of these lines might work!

Smooth Talker: *"If I buy you another drink right now, will you forget that I said that?"*

Ditz: *"Oops, did I say something stupid? So sorry! Just strike that remark from the record!"*

The Interrogator: *"Have I been too nosy? I'll shut up now."*

Shy Girl: *"Please forgive me. That was so insensitive."*

The Helper : *"I deeply apologize if I've hurt your feelings. I am such a blunderer!"*

Comedienne: *"Obviously I just goofed. Wanna join me in the bathroom while I wash my mouth out with soap?"*

If you play this right, he might soon be apologizing to you! Actually, that's great flirting!

His Body Language: What's He *Really* Saying?

You've been trading witticisms with this guy for fifteen or twenty minutes. That he's still hanging with you makes it obvious that he's enjoying himself. But how do you know if you're going to be swapping spit later or if he considers you just a pleasant diversion until the Real Thing arrives? Get a read on his body language to help you figure it out!

Action: He's leaning his elbows on the table starin' straight at ya.

Meaning: He's warm to you. Keep on doing whatever you're doing. It's working to heat things up!

Action: He is fiddling with his napkin, tearing it into bits.

Meaning: He's trying to distract himself because something about you is making him nervous. The good kind of nervous! If you can sneak a peek down there, check out his package. Telltale bulge or not?

Action: His cell phone rang but he put the caller on Ignore. His cell phone rings again. This time he picks it up and says to the caller, "Can I call you back? I'm busy."

Meaning: Bingo! This means that he'd rather talk to you than—her!

Action: He's leaning way back in his chair.

Meaning: This means he's trying to keep a little distance. He may find you superattractive but if his girlfriend were to walk in right now, he knows he's gonna hear about it.

Action: He keeps going for his drink.

Meaning: This means his mouth is dry . . . did you cause that to happen?

Now that you feel pretty confident that you're getting to him, i.e., getting under his skin, introduce a little body language of your own just to get a pulse on where exactly things are headed. For example, if you touch his hand or his forearm, does he move it away? If you slide your chair closer does he also move his a little closer?

After you try these moves out and he's still hanging with it, here's some tips on how not to blow it:

Don't fiddle with your napkin. You don't want him to see that he's making you sweat.

Do encourage him by giving him little fleeting glimpses of flesh.

Don't lean toward him if you're sharing a table. In fact, scoot away a bit. Now is the time for you to create some distance. Make him come to you!

Do feed him food with your hands.

Don't lick your lips or fiddle with your hair. It's too early to give away how hot he's making you.

Do say his name often (men love to hear their name).

Don't start babbling. You've come so far measuring out your words, don't blow it by revealing your inner chatterbox.

Do take a break from the conversation by applying more lipstick. Men find this to be terribly hot!

Don't change flirting styles midstream. If he's been responding so well to your Shy Girl, don't confuse him now by suddenly turning into a Ditz.

Do depart while he's obviously lusting after you. Do know that he's watching your rear as you leave.

Escalating the Sexed-Up Factor

Things are heating up between the two of you and suddenly the conversation has jumped into another play zone. The chemistry and the pheromones between you two are really flying. You want to get the message across that you find him to be an extra special attractive person, even a potential bedmate—but what can you say without sounding sluttish? It goes back to the use of the double entendre we talked about earlier in this book.

As you surely know by now, certain words have an amazing effect on men. Because a guy's mind is hardwired to work a mile a minute toward sex, just about any word you say that sounds even a little bit filthy will get him excited. When you're really ready to turn up the temperature, try dipping back into your bag of double entendres. If you deliver them very sweetly and with no hint of sly erotic inflection, they're doubly potent!

* At a cocktail/preview party where caterers are circulating around with loaded trays: "Hey, *snatch* me another drink."
* Patting the seat next to you on the couch: *Squeeze* in here right next to me.
* When the credits are coming up at the end of a movie: That really *touched* me.
* Playing with a bit of string with your kitten: Here, *Pussy*!

PUTTIN' THE PEDAL TO THE METAL

Here are hardcore pickup artist lines for the boldest of flirts.

* "Why don't you come over here . . . like, right now?"
* "I pick you."
* "You just said you have a girlfriend? So what?"
* "Nobody ever says no to me."
* "My breasts? They're real."
* "You can touch me if you want to. But only where I say so."
* "Do you mind if I take you home with me right now?"
* "Is it a big deal to you that I'm not wearing panties?"

Uh-Oh. Why Is He Looking at Me That Way?

Is he falling for you big time . . . or is he clingy?

There are looks from guys . . . and there are looks. Some guys—even really cute ones—are so desperate that they'll go after any girl who gives them any attention. This behavior may seem flattering at first, but it's not real. It's based on the guy's insecurities or whatever isn't immediately visible to the eye regarding what the hell is wrong with him.

Telltale Signs That You've Got a Clinger

Just like there will be signs a guy's interested, a guy who obviously is into you can also give off signs that something's not quite right—and no one wants to get caught up with a clinger. If he exhibits any of the actions below—get out fast!

* It's only been ten minutes but he's already talking to you like you're his girlfriend.
* He keeps moving his hand toward your lap. It's starting to get annoying now.
* He's attentive. Too attentive.
* He asks you if you'd like to have kids and then tells you all his favorite names.
* He won't let go of your elbow.
* When he has to visit the men's room, he asks you to go with him.
* He won't let you out of his sight.
* He's drooling.

Go Ahead, Be a Bitch.

Being a bitch can be a very powerful thing. If you're trying to ditch the dreaded clinger, try employing some of your best bitchy lines can get rid of him . . . fast.

Bitchy lines to get rid of the Clinger:

* "I never was that into you but now I'm so over you."
* "What was that you said, little boy?"
* "You're talking to *ME*?"
* "Take a hike, Mike."
* "Don't call me."

On the other hand, some guys respond very excitedly to women who bully them, and you can use this to your advantage in certain situations. Warning: Shy Girls need not apply for this job. If you're not brazen by nature, channel your inner dominatrix to deliver these devastating verbal doozies.

* "You want me to smack you?"
* "Down, boy, down!"
* "You think you can get away with that?"
* "One more time now, just one more time."
* "Are you challenging me?"
* "You are sooo out of line."

When you say these words to a certain type of man, don't be surprised if he doesn't immediately make a grab for you!

The great majority of guys, however, prefer women who are

only partially a bitch. Remember that most men think anything a woman asks of them is really a demand? That's their way of saying she's "high maintenance"! Guys really respect high-maintenance women and can quickly develop the hots for them. So if you want to be a little high maintenance, follow this advice:

✳   Be a smart mouth—have an answer for everything.

✳   Don't be timid—if you want something, ask for it!

✳   Be confident—men love a confident woman.

✳   Don't equivocate—be decisive.

✳   Be a little late for everything—men expect to wait, especially for a beautiful woman!

WORK IT: TEN LINES TO INSTANTLY BOOST HIS CONFIDENCE

✳   "I think you are so clever. Tell me what you said one more time?"

✳   "Your last girlfriend said your ears are too big? I think your ears are adorable!"

✳   "I could have never figured that out. How'd you do it?"

✳   "I don't think I've ever met anyone with better taste than you."

✳   "Unbelievable car! Take me for a ride?"

✳   "This is your house? Wow, you must make a lot of money."

✳   "I don't really care what a guy looks like if I admire his mind."

* "You got tickets to————? You must be connected!"
* "Your mother did a great job with you. You have the most beautiful manners."
* "You seem so well traveled."

Chapter Six

The Pickup Artist

So once you've got him where you want him (i.e., in a conversation), how do you interpret what he's saying and use it to your advantage?

In this chapter you will learn the secrets of deciphering and decoding common male linguistic subterfuges and techniques as well as tactics to help you direct a conversation where *you* want it to go! You'll also learn the conversational gambits necessary to turn you into a supersleuth so that you'll know exactly who and what you're talking to! Is he married or single? A relationship guy or a player? Or is he a little bit of both?

Analyze This

Most women find talking to guys very frustrating because they try too hard to look for meaning in what he's saying. For example, if he says, "I love dancing," does he mean it or did he only say it because he thinks the woman will like him better? Or was he being sarcastic? Depending on a man's tone of voice, inflection, a particular emphasis on a word, any simple statement coming out of a man's mouth can suddenly mean . . . lots of things.

It's not that you're hard of hearing or extraordinarily dense, but the fact of the matter is, most guys are really a chore to talk to. For as much time as women spend thinking about guys, most of us aren't really fluent in the language of *guy*, and this leaves you little choice except to leave your standard conversational comfort zone. Unless you're fortunate to have grown up in a family of several sons and you're totally fluent in football or golf or baseball or the dreaded videogames, you're probably going to have to do some boning up.

At this point you may be sighing and thinking you'll just stick talking to gay guys since at least they'll talk hair and gossip. But don't give up so quickly. Part of becoming a master flirtress is looking and listening carefully—read on to learn more!

First, you've got to be a bit of a conversational detective. Your goal is to pick up on conversational leads he unconsciously sends out, so that you can direct the conversation any way you want it to go. Another perk of mastering the art of picking up conversation is that it guarantees you'll never run out of topics. All you have to do is listen to what he's saying and then pick out specific words or phrases that naturally lend themselves to furthering the communication—and at the same time possibly gain you additional info.

For example, say you're sitting at a bar with him and he's telling you about his work. He tells you he loves his job but dislikes the commute. You pick up on the word "commute," and ask him how long it takes, what roads he drives. Through his answer, you now have a fair idea of where he lives, even though he didn't tell you directly.

Active Listening

You'll be able to glean important conversational tidbits through active listening. Active listening is a way of listening with energy.

When you actively listen to someone you try to go beyond the actual words they are saying to get to a deeper meaning. For example, if the guy tells you he rarely goes home for Christmas, you can pick up on any tone of regret or hostility or pain in his voice, however slight or subtle, and then go straight in for the emotional impact question, which would be something along the lines of, "Is there a problem with your visiting your family?" If he answers, be prepared to settle in for a long listen. This is the type of conversation that jumpstarts (sometimes too rapidly) Level Four Intimacy (more on that soon).

Do's and Don'ts for Sharing

Do share amusing intimacies, such as your genetic heritage of receiving the famous family "ticklish gene."

Don't reveal that your aunt passed away in an asylum—unless the guy you're sharing with is sitting beside you in group therapy. Now, that could lead to real bonding!

Do share preferences for light, trivial topics, like your favorite flavor of ice cream or a weakness for mochachinos. Not every shared intimacy has to be earth-shattering.

Don't kiss and tell. If the subject is old boyfriends/girlfriends, don't share their personal sexual preferences or secrets. That's just plain offensive.

Do share travel stories, volunteer work that you've done, anything that allows him to know you're out and about in the world. You might discover that both of you vacationed in Negril at the same time two years ago.

Don't hesitate to play that game of "six degrees of separation." This is a real theory developed in 1929 by the Hungarian writer Frigyes Karinthy in a short story he wrote called "Chains." Six degrees of separation says that anyone on the planet can be connected to any other person on the planet through a chain of acquaintances that has no more than five intermediaries. It does seem true that if you ask people where they went to school, what town they grew up in; in what branch of military service they served; their church or synagogue affiliation; and about their membership in private clubs, professional organizations, fraternities or sororities, chances are that you know some person in common.

Stuff You Can Say to Lull Him into Feeling Comfortable with You

You don't have to have the Helper personality to intuit what you can say to a man to make him feel more comfortable (i.e., open) toward you. Try these lines to make him safe and cozy:

* "Omigod, that's so awful. I feel so terrible for you. Tell me again, your boss/teacher/person who works in the cubicle next to you said what?"

* "My family drives me batshit, too. But what can you do about it?"

* "You look like you could use a beer. Why don't you sit right next to me and have one?"

* "Rough day? Tell me about it."

* "Go ahead. Whine to me. You'll feel better for it."

* "You look like you've been run ragged. Sit down. Take a load off."

* "Hey, sugar. Come and tell mama all your itty-bitty problems."

Should You Stay or Should You Go?

There will be moments when you'll be talking to a guy and suddenly a lightbulb goes on. You have a moment of important insight. Sure, he's good looking. But if he displays even one of the following signs, dump his ass—quick!

* He licks his lips the whole time he's talking to you. This is very bad. He's sending you every kind of signal that he's hungry for whatever and intends to eat you up! This is also known as Big Bad Wolf syndrome.
* He seems sleepy, very sleepy. Is he on drugs?
* He keeps leaving your side to make a private phone call. What is he? Married? Or just up to no good?
* He receives ten phone calls or pages within an hour. Face it, babe. He's just too busy for you.
* He keeps borrowing your cell phone.
* He eats off your plate not because it's cute and sexy but because he just wants your food.
* He looks in his wallet and he looks dismayed.
* He won't stop talking about his mother.
* He tells you about his cat . . . *all* about his cat.
* He says he hates dogs, and you've got one.
* He mentions his last girlfriend's name and starts crying.
* He can't remember his name.
* He can't remember where he parked the car.
* His car will not start.
* It's a nice restaurant but he's wearing gym shorts.
* He tells you his favorite celebrity is a porn star.
* He asks if you ever "take it out in trade."

* His brother is in jail. He thinks his dad might be in jail, too.
* He says he's been married before . . . like five times.
* You invite him to stay over but he says he has to call home first.
* His socks don't match. They smell pretty rank, too.
* He makes cracks about fat girls.
* You invite him for dinner and he shows up at the door with cheap wine. Like, *really* cheap wine.
* He says he hates his mother. This is the worst. No matter how great he seems to you right now, understand that guys who hate their mothers will in no time start hating *you!*

WHAT'S IN A HAT?

Hats are a mating signal, a call, a summons for finding a like mate. Until you became a flirting expert, you probably paid scant attention to male headgear. But what a man chooses to wear on his head says volumes about his lifestyle, his preferences, his choices. So the next time you're thinking of approaching a guy, take notice of his hat. Is it emblazoned with the words "Denver Broncos," "Lone Star Feed & Grain," or "Budweiser"? There's a reason guys wear those hats, and it's not just cuz their hair is thinning.

Study up on this quick guide to what different hats mean, to give you get more insight into this person!

Baseball hat: This is the universal hat for guys who are balding or who are really into their favorite teams.

Good line to say here: "You love the Bulls? You must be from Chicago."

Beret: Only an authentic French guy can really pull this off. Any other man wearing it just looks like he's trying to emulate a Beat poet. Which, come to think of it, may not necessarily be a bad thing . . .
Good line to say here: "Are you French?"

Do-rag: This headgear is hot and sexy on black guys. A white boy in a do-rag is suspect, to say the least!
Good line to say here: "Are you a fan of hip-hop or are you just making a fashion statement?"

Fedora: This isn't your grandfather's hat any longer! Guys who wear this hat are usually older or old-fashioned. A younger guy who wears it probably pays good attention to detail— after all, he's cultivating a great retro look by wearing it! Steal this hat. It'll probably look better on *you*.
Good line to say here: "I love your hat? Can I borrow it?"

Fur bomber: Is he a model . . . or a bicycle messenger?
Good line to say here: "That hat looks so amazing on you. Is it Dolce and Gabbana?"

Motorcycle helmet. Vrooom-vroom, baby!
Good line to say here: "Where's your bike?"

Stetson: Unless this guy's from Texas, this is a pretty affected hat. On the other hand, it's pretty sexy . . . especially if you have a little fetish thing working about cowboys.
Good line to say here: "That chapeau is a real head turner. Is it hand blocked?"

Reindeer antlers: Very funny . . . but only around Christmas.
Great line to say here: "Aren't you adorable?" Or "Where's Rudolph?"

Wool cap: This is a great preppy look . . . or just something a day laborer wears.
Great line to say here. "That hat looks so warm. Is it?"

Your Top Secret Male Decoder System—How to Know What He's *Really* Saying

We've already said that there are all kinds of ways guys choose to communicate with women in a possible pickup situation. So much depends on the male personality type. For example, a shy guy might try to utter as few words as possible, preferring the woman take the conversational lead, whereas a superconfident alpha male might be turned off if the female makes the first move. Here are a few tips on how to handle different male speaking styles and make the most of any situation.

The Mumbler

He's really cute but he's a bit of a marble-mouth! This kind of guy is phobic about committing to the spoken word. Usually it's because his words have gotten him into trouble before with the ladies, so he chooses to speak so softly or unintelligibly that no woman can understand what he's saying. Mumbling guys are often quite shy.

How to deal: Part of the Mumbler's flirting style is to get a reaction. If you say to him, "Excuse me?" now you're talking. You could also pretend that you understand him and just say "Yes, yes," to everything he says. Remember—if you're into him, it's better to charm the Mumbler than to chide him. Even if his behavior brings out the latent Perfect Enunciator in you, ignore any impulse to correct him, or you'll risk driving him away.

The Talk-Around-in-Circles Guy

When you're around this guy, you don't know if you're coming or going. He's like a car salesman. Even if you can keep up with him, ultimately you'll just find him annoying. These guys tend to wear jewelry. Lots of it! They also tend to talk with their hands.

How to deal: Try to bring this guy in for a landing. Get him to focus. But that won't be easy. If that doesn't work, play with him. Play him like a yo-yo. You can also try to tire him out. Run him ragged by asking him a lot of questions. Then sock it to him and ask something really important, like "So, how many kids do you have?"

The Fast Talker

We all know a fast talker. He's slick. Sometimes he's good looking, in a sharklike kind of way, but just as often the main thing he's got going for him is he has a lot of nerve. Fast talkers will talk (and flirt!) rings around you. Watch out.

How to deal: Even if you're a talker, too, the best way to deal with this guy is to tone down the talking. Sometimes you have to let a guy like this just talk himself out. Remember to maintain eye contact. That keeps a connection going. Don't give up even if it seems he's never going to be quiet. He has to stop sometime, just to take a sip of something—or breathe.

The Incommunicado Guy

This guy has made an art out of saying as little as possible. You have no idea what he's thinking because he prefers it that way. For some reason women find this guy sexy and mysterious. His withholding of words conjures up images of the Marlboro Man or some other great iconic western figure. Most of these guys say as little as possible because all they really want to say is, "When are you going to get naked?"

How to deal: The Incommunicado Guy doesn't care if you talk or not. Words to him are a matter of complete indifference. Just understand that this guy probably just wants to get you into bed and—he doesn't like pillow talk, either!

The Joker

The Joker is a party boy. He likes having fun. He's a good-time guy to hang out with, he's generous, he's always surrounded by people, he has a lot of friends, but who is this guy, anyway? What's behind his boys-just-wanna-have-fun persona?

How to deal: If you want to curry this guy's favor, beware of stepping on his lines or in any way upstaging him. On the other hand, if you want to annoy him or pull his chain, get up on a chair and do your own comedy routine, Ms. Comedienne.

If you do want to get a little insight into who this guy really is, channel your inner Helper and ask him a few personal questions, like "When did you learn to be so funny, anyway?" Just remember, for these characters, laughter and jokes often cover up something dark and dispirited. It's easy to fall in love with this kind of guy, but watch out. He can be trouble.

The Arguer

This guy loves nothing more than a good verbal sparring match, which can be really fun for an outspoken, flirtatious woman. However, proceed with caution—the Arguer can be stubborn, and your conversation could go from flirt to flat in under a minute if you touch upon the wrong subject. He's known to close out one of his "discussions" with the words, "I'm not simplistic. I'm right."

How to deal: The Arguer is often (sigh) a lawyer. He enjoys debate and repartee the way other guys enjoy a Coors Light. Arguers get on well with other Arguers, so go ahead and give it back to him, Interrogator girl!

The Fact Spouter

This is the guy who feels compelled to back everything he says up with "facts." He doesn't trust himself to be spontaneous. He has to go in with a script. A large portion of his conversational gambits and stories, he gleans off the Internet: He's great at regaling his friends and future dates with trivia he has picked up on The Smoking Gun and other investigative sites he clicked on just that day. Take him by surprise by spouting some facts of your own . . . and then watch how he reacts!

How to deal: The Fact Spouter has to be thrown off his usual self-imposed script, or you'll never get to know what he's really like at all! The best way to handle this guy is to absorb his spouting for a few minutes and then change the subject to something you hope he doesn't have an arsenal of information about. Without the protective armor of his facts to hide behind, the guy will have to actually talk to you.

The Have-to-Get-the-Last-Word-In-er

This guy is tough. Very likely, he's a lawyer. He can be smug to the point of being unctuous. It is fun to throw him for a loop by making sure *you* get in the last word.

How to deal: The Have-to-Get-the-Last-Word-In-er can be handled two ways. The first is to beat him at his own game by quickly responding wittily to everything he says. This is a good position to take if you happen to be a natural Smooth Talker yourself. Another choice that works very well is to quickly adopt the stance of a Shy Girl and say nothing. Let the guy talk himself out and then move in for the kill.

The Gossipy Guy

This guy is tremendously entertaining even if you're somewhat horrified by what comes out of his mouth. He's hilarious, often snide; he's really a blast to be seated next to at any dinner party because all the things he whispers to you as an aside are just delicious dish. Just remember that the Gossipy Guy is very likely to talk about *you* as soon as you're out of earshot. So be careful what you say to him, because he'll repeat it. Unless he's your wingman and best friend, you can't really trust him!

How to deal: The Gossipy Guy is the the ideal companion for all Comediennes. Well-matched wise-acres, they might be a dream couple. No other woman will really appreciate this snappy sort of guy, so if you meet one and he's not for you, pass him along to one of your funny girlfriends.

The Whiner

Something's always bothering the Whiner, and he's not afraid to let you know about it! Maybe he's had a bad day at work, or his back hurts, or he has a cold. But whatever it is—rest assured he'll let you know about it—even if you've just met him. Incredibly, some major hotties are also major whiners. They must learn it at their mother's feet. These guys do have their own special charm, though, especially if you're Jewish.

How to deal: Whiner guys are an acquired taste. Women either love them or hate them. Jerry Seinfeld and Larry David (the "Curb Your Enthusiasm" guy) are classic whiners. They do respect and worship authoritative women, so don't hesitate to tell a whiner when to shut up. Just smile at him when you say it.

A great tactic to use when wooing a Whiner is just to let him whine himself out. Helper girls should turn on their most sympathetic charm, while Shy girls can sit quietly until he runs out of things to moan about. The ultimate trick with a Whiner is to get him to laugh. Comediennes can point out the humor in anything the Whiner is whining about.

The Boaster

You know him. He can't stop applauding himself, and he usually surrounds himself with a throng of admirers—both male and female. As long as you're willing to jump on the bandwagon and boast about him too, he'll think you walk on water!

How to deal: Boasters are such conversational self-starters that part of their charm is the women who are with them don't have to say much. If you find yourself falling for a Boaster guy, just cultivate your most enraptured smile and he'll think you're his biggest fan.

The Cheerleader

This guy loves to cheer on everybody but himself. He's a one-man fan club for his friends and everyone's favorite wingman. When it comes to themselves, however, these guys are usually painfully modest.

How to deal: The Cheerleader is really such a shy guy that he needs a woman who will derail him from talking about everybody else and who forces him to talk about himself. Helper girls can work wonders with Cheerleaders . . . the danger is that they do such a good job that the dude turns into a Boaster . . . eeech.

The Documentarian

This guy is a chronicler. He has to tell you about all his past loves, the first time he had sex, every detail about his first crush. Be aware that if you get involved with him, you'll become part of his chronology. Think hard before you fall for a Documentarian. Do you really want to be another notch on this record-keeper's belt?

How to deal: The Documentarian is best dealt with by a Smooth Talking woman who sweetly lets him know that she isn't interested in being just another statistic and that if he insists on talking about all his former conquests, she's out the door.

The Love-the-Sound-of-My-Own-Voice Guy

This man talks just to hear himself speaking. His voice isn't the only thing he loves about himself.

How to deal: Love-the-Sound-of-His-Own-Voice Guys are best handled by women who love the sound of that guy's voice. If you want to be with this man, you better enjoy listening to him.

The What Guy

This guy says "What?" or "Wha?" to almost everything you say. Very little children do this to provoke their mothers. Is this the relationship you envision?

How to deal: The What Guy is best just ignored. There is no point in talking to him. It doesn't matter what you say. Your every utterance will be responded to with a "Wha?" If he's cute enough and you want to jump him, don't let this little language barrier between you become a major problem.

The Droner

This guy just drones on and on. After a while you don't even hear what he's saying. Just for the fun of it, see if you can interrupt him. Odds are on you can't.

How to deal: The Droner can be very exhausting to hang with. Most women's first impulse upon encountering such a guy is to run away from him. Sometimes it's best to follow one's impulses. But if you think he's really cute or would be cute if he would just shut up, tell him to stick a sock in it or shut his mouth by kissing him into silence . . .

The Performer

This guy is the life of the party . . . up to a certain point. After you run into him at a few events/functions, you'll detect that he's more of an actor than a real human being. He may be an amazing storyteller but after a while you realize that every tale is a set piece.

How to deal: The Performer does best with a woman whose conversational style is that she likes to perform, too. Performers of both sexes are often very entertaining and are fun to hang out with, but be aware that when you're in the company of a Performer, you're going to hear the same material over and over again.

The Apologizer

Poor fellow. This is the guy who is sorry for everything. If he's two minutes late, he apologizes about it. If the waiter is slow to bring the menu, he apologizes. He apologizes about the seats he got at a concert. He just can't stop saying he's sorry to the point where you want to shout, "That's enough!"

How to deal: Helper girls are really good with this type of guy. They understand that what's called for is to be kind and sympathetic. There are certain women for whom a man's saying "I'm sorry," is music to their ears. Hey, it takes all kinds.

Getting the Goods

Once you've employed active listening and determined what type of guy you're dealing with, the next step in your flirtation education is refining your skills in what is known as the fine art of "getting the goods." What are "the goods," you ask? In a nutshell, these are the kinds of things you'd really like to ask a guy you just met, if you could be totally candid. Unfortunately, basic manners and current codes of decency prohibit asking rude questions of perfect strangers, unless you're a journalist by profession and then it's your business to ask nosy questions—and expect answers, too! Here's what you want to know:

* *His marital/engaged/relationship status.* Is he or isn't he available?
* *Where does he live?* While sharing the same zip code does give you something in common, it's also fun to flirt with someone who is just visiting from out of town. If you know you'll probably never see this guy again, you can really cut loose and play with him. Think of it as a flirt freebie . . .
* *What's he driving?* Of course this is shallow, but cars do tell so much about a person.
* *Sexual compatibility quotient?* Sure, he's cute enough, but can he only get his thrills from smearing you all over with peanut butter or is he likely to tie you up?
* *What's his fiscal situation?* His spending habits say a lot about him. Is he flashy or stingy? Is he responsible or reckless?
* *The deal breakers.* Drugs? Booze? Pills? Does he have any habit or problem that you need to know about right now?

These five points cover what one might call the obvious questions. How do you get the info you need before you get in too deep? Whether you decide to get the goods by playing either the disingenuous charmer or the smooth sleuth, remember these aren't the type of questions you can normally ask out of the box. Try and get to know him for a few minutes before springing it all on him . . . if only to lull him into a sense of security so that you catch him out off guard!

His Relationship Status

Try on these different lines to determine his availability status (he'll never be the wiser):

* ✳   "Hmm. You're not wearing a ring. How can I tell if you're married?"
* ✳   "Your clothes are so well taken care of. Do you do it or does somebody else do it for you?"
* ✳   "You have a wife, a girlfriend, you're living with someone . . . come on. What's your story?"
* ✳   "A guy as cute/sexy/funny as you surely is spoken for, right?"
* ✳   "You're quite a catch. Has somebody caught you?"
* ✳   "Is your girlfriend going to get mad that you're out so late? Or would that be your mother?"

Where Does He Live?

Is he a neighbor or an out-of-towner? Here are some quickie lines you can use to extract helpful geographical info.

* ✳   "How many freeway exits exactly are you from here?"
* ✳   "Are you far from home?"

✳ "Now where do I know that accent from? Could it be you're from Philadelphia?"

✳ "Come around often?"

✳ "Where'd you get that tan? I got mine at that little place around the corner."

✳ "What's your zip code?"

What's He Driving

You can tell a lot about a guy by his car. Here are some easy lines to help you out.

✳ "You don't look like a guy familiar with public transportation. So, tell me what are you're drivin'?"

✳ "I love Beamers. You haven't got one, have you?"

✳ "I might need a lift. Do you have a car?"

✳ "Gearshifts and brakes and stuff like that have always baffled me. I don't even have my license."

✳ "Let me guess. You look like a Subaru kind of person."

Your Sexual Compatibility Quotient

You're really attracted to this guy and you want to let him know it. But how wild is he? Try one of these sexy lines to find out.

✳ "You're not the kind of guy who goes in for blindfolds and French ticklers, are you?"

✳ "I'm not kinky. Are you kinky?"

✳ "I love a guy who will rub me and rub me for hours. You wouldn't happen to be a masseur, would you?"

✳ "Water sports? You mean like, water polo?"

* "You groove on women who wear tall black boots? Me, too, unless you ask me to walk on you."

His Fiscal Situation

You don't need Donald Trump to make you happy, but you don't want to get stuck with Ebenezer Scrooge, either. These lines will help you flush out his spending ways.

* "Are you getting this round?"
* "Is that your wallet?"
* "I only carry credit cards. How about you?"
* "Did I hear you say 'Dutch treat'?"
* "Is there a reason you've mentioned three times how broke you are?"

The Deal Breakers

If you're really into him, it's best to get any potential relationship destroying stuff out of the way as quickly as possible, right?

* "What is that white stuff coming out of your nose?"
* "You've been using the restroom a lot. What's happening in there?"
* "Boy, you're slim. Is that because you do heroin or because you don't eat?"
* "Do you always wear long sleeves?"
* "That pale, hollow look? Did you purposely cultivate it?"
* "You're talking awfully fast. Are you high or something?"

SAMPLE SCRIPTS TO HELP YOU GET THE GOODS

If you're still looking for easy ways to get information from him, you can tailor any of these sample scripts to your situation.

Factoid you want to find out: How old is he?

Smooth Talker: "The Pogues? You saw them live? When?"

Interrogator: "Um, so how old are you, anyway?"

Comedienne: "Your mother watched *Melrose Place* with you when you were a little kid?"

Shy Girl: "I never can tell anybody's age. Everybody says I look about sixteen."

Factoid you want to find out: Does he have a roommate?

Comedienne: "My roommate is amazing but I just wish she'd stop doing all our laundry. She just doesn't grasp the concept of 'hand wash.'"

Interrogator: "Do you think you'd ever consider a roommate?"

Smooth Talker: "I love seeing how single guys decorate. Is there a poster of Britney over your bed?"

Shy Girl: "If I had my own place I think I'd get a pet."

Helper: "I really enjoy my private time at home. What about you?"

Factoid you want to find out: Does he have a girlfriend?

Shy Girl: "I'm not seeing anyone special right now."

Comedienne: "A guy like you must have a girlfriend."

Helper: "Are you in a relationship?"

Smooth Talker: "Are you dating anyone seriously or are you just into messing around?"

Interrogator: "Are you dating anyone?"

SAMPLE SCRIPTS FOR GETTING HIM TO POP THE QUESTION (NOT *THAT* QUESTION!)

Sometimes you just want to get him to ask you out, if not on an actual date, at least something that might lead toward one. Try these meaningful (!) dialogues to help push things in that direction.

He: "Hey, I was just going to go out for some coffee. Want to come?"
She: "Darn, I can't tear myself away from my desk right now. What about later?"

He: "You look great in that outfit."
She: "Thanks! All dressed up and no place to go. Got any ideas?"

He: "We should get together sometime."
She: "Fantastic. What are you doing later?"

Is He *Really* Available?

Guys who technically are available, i.e., they're not married or living with someone, sometimes give mixed messages about their true availabilty status. It takes a little probing to find out if they're serious about their relationship. He may be open to having a fling, but are you?

He's probably available if:

* He doesn't care what time he gets home.
* He answers or at least looks at his cell phone when it's ringing.
* He asks you what you're doing later.
* He readily offers his last name.
* He asks for your phone number.
* He says he comes around this place a lot.
* He says he lives in the neighborhood.
* He gives you his number if you ask for it.
* He hands you his card.
* He asks if you come here often.
* He asks if you want to hook up.

Is He Taken?

A guy who is truly taken may or may not flirt with you. It all depends on his internal moral code—or that of his wife or girlfriend. Many very married men have been given permission by their wives to verbally flirt a little. But that's as far as they'll go. His wife doesn't mind because she's probably the flirty type, too. But how can you tell if he's flirting for fun . . . or trolling for real trouble?

He's probably *not* available if:

* He keeps looking at the time because he's supposed to be someplace else . . . with someone else.
* He won't answer his phone even though it keeps ringing.
* He doesn't offer his card.

* He puts your number in his phone's memory but won't let you type his into yours.
* He says he'll call you because it's "inconvenient" for you to call him.
* He gives you only his work number.
* He acts as if he has no last name.
* He invites you to meet him somewhere . . . three towns over.
* He says he's married but makes sure to comment, "There are problems."

Waving the Red Flag

Some guys who will flirt up a storm with you make it very difficult to tell if they're single or taken. A woman has to look and listen very hard to read the signals. If there's a lot of chemistry happening, lust will make this task even murkier. Take a look at this list of red flags to keep you on your toes.

He's *definitely not* available if:

* He answers his phone and a toddler is shrieking in the background.
* That's Play Doh, not paint, under his fingernails.
* You asked him what he did for Halloween and he said he went trick-or-treating.
* He says he's never free on the weekends.
* He only available on weeknights.
* He says he can only come over to your place.
* He says his wife lets him date.

He's So Cute, but Is He Straight or Gay?

You've been talking to this guy for half an hour and he's so easy to talk to. He's good looking and attentive, and he likes discussing all the things you like to discuss—even clothes. You can't believe it, but the two of you have been chattering away like a pair of magpies about designer labels. He's looking into your eyes and smiling, which you take to be a signal of interest, but when you slipped off into the ladies' room to apply more lipstick, your best friend told you that she thinks he's gay! Without directly asking (and risking alienating him forever!), how do you find out if he's into guys or girls?

While there are no absolute signs that say a guy is gay unless he's wearing a T-shirt that says so, there are clues and signals. Memorize this short list of He's Gay/He's Not Gay notes and see how they apply to your object of flirtation.

He's probably gay if:

* He's carrying the latest issues of *GQ, and Men's Health.*
* He mentions someone he recently traveled with and somehow manages to evade mentioning the person's gender.
* He is superfinicky about the way he spreads his napkin. Like, superfinicky.
* He has a black Scottie dog he calls "Mr. Smith."
* He smiles at you and laughs at your jokes, but his eyes never follow your bottom when you leave the room.

He's definitely not gay if:

* He tells you there's a condom in his wallet.

* He asks for your phone number, your screen name, and your e-mail address.
* When he thinks you're not listening, he whispers to his buddy, "She's hot."

Is He Lying? Listen to His Body Language

There's an old saying among real estate agents: "Buyers are liars." What that means in Realtor parlance is that buyers rarely tell the truth. They say they can only afford to spend blah-blah-blah when really they can spend more, or they claim they can only be happy in a Colonial but wind up buying a split level. It's the real estate agent's task to figure out the truth in what any buyer says. The same holds true for women when they're dealing with men. Men, like home buyers, are liars. Here's how to suss out the real story!

Body language is a big (although not the biggest) giveaway when you're trying to determine the veracity of what another person is saying. Here are some clues to guide you:

* *Lack of eye contact.* A guy who won't look you in the eye is a guy who is trying to hide or get away with something! Don't believe a word this one says!
* *Gestures don't match the verbal statement.* If there's a serious disconnect between what's coming out of his mouth and his physical language, you're definitely dealing with a liar . . . or someone who is way out of touch with his own emotions. For example, a guy who scowls or frowns

as he's telling you how crazy he is about you is either not really into you at all—or he's so miserable that is he falling for you, that you'd better watch out. Either way – run! Run for the hills!

* *The fake smile.* A fake smile is one where only the muscles around the mouth move. If his eyes aren't smiling even though his lips are curled up, you're dealing with a liar.

* *He turns his head away when he's talking to you.* This can mean two things. The first is he's not really paying attention to you. The other is that he is looks as if he's paying attention but he doesn't actually want to hear what you're saying. Either way, he's not being honest in how he's relating to you!

* *He puts something physical between you.* You're sitting at a table with him and he keeps moving the salt shaker or his coffee cup or the plant on the table between you. When a man sets up a physical barrier between himself and a woman, it means he's putting up a wall. Ask yourself why he is doing this?

* *Lip licking, trouser adjusting, weight shifting, foot jiggling, blinking, and pivoting.* These are all classic physical signals that a person is feeling nervous or anxious. Although these tics and motions aren't absolute signals that a guy is lying, if you happen to be asking him a direct question and he does this, chances are he's being dishonest.

Verbal Cues That Tell You He's Lying

Contrary to popular belief, body language is not the most serious indicator that someone's not telling the truth. Often deceit is more easily determined by the words a person says, or how he picks and chooses them.

✱ *He uses a lot of contractions.* A contraction is "almost" truthful. Saying "Didn't do it," is not as emphatic as "I did not do it."

✱ *He avoids direct statements.* He says he went to the movies last night . . . but doesn't say what film. You ask him if he's got a girlfriend and he says, "Not really." What do you think is going on here?

✱ *He heaps details and embellishments on to his story.* Liars tend to go overboard telling a story. All these extras are meant to bolster his lie and make it seem more "real."

✱ *He garbles his words or speaks very softly.* When a guy talks like this, it means he hopes you don't really hear him! His hope is that if you catch him in an out-and-out lie, he can always say you misheard or misunderstood him!

✱ *There are long pauses between his sentences.* This means he's thinking real hard about what he is saying. He may be trying to trick you! His game here is that he's trying to stay one step ahead, so you'll have a harder time sussing him out.

✱ *His words are overconfident.* Smooth Talking liars are easy to spot. When a guy relies on stock phrases like "I've got you covered," usually it means just the opposite!

✱ *Dissociation.* He talks about himself in the third person. He introduces himself as "Benny the Cat," and then talks about "the Cat" all night instead of saying the words "me" or "I." This is superslick and can be very funny, but it's also a way of being dishonest.

What About the Guy Whose Favorite Phrase Is "No Problem"?

So you're talking to a guy who repeats the phrase "no problem" more than a couple of times during your conversation. This can be a good thing—or a bad thing. How to interpret the meaning of his repeated use of this idiom? Some "No Problem" guys are terrific because they really mean it. Nothing is a big problem to them, or, if there is a problem (say, you just locked yourself out of your car) they know how to fix it. This kind of guy is a problem solver, which is a great kind of guy to have around.

On the other hand, a guy who says "no problem" a lot can be a big ball of trouble, because he's the guy who regularly blows things off. His ease of saying "no problem," may be a mask to cover up the fact that he's really irresponsible but good at making excuses for himself. Beware the "No Problem" guy, because he might have a lot of problems!

The Four Levels of Intimacy

If you're still talking to this guy, you must want to be learning a little more about him—*him*, the person, not just that hunky or adorable man toy you met fifteen minutes ago over by the guacamole.

By using the Four Levels of Intimacy, you can ramp up the conversation to another level by introducing topics that lead to sharing. Sharing happens in increments ranging from tantalizing tidbits straight through to full-bore autobiography . . . the uncensored, uncut version.

Level One: Tidbits

This is the entry-level stage of sharing. This is personal, but not too personal things one person can tell another person about themselves. Good tidbit topics are birth order, level of education, who you might know in common, and places you've visited or lived in.

* "I'm the baby in my family, can't you tell?"
* "Neither of my parents went to college. I'm the first one."
* "I'll probably have a big family because I come from one. Do you have brothers and sisters?"
* "I've been doing a lot of thinking about grad school. Is it for me?"
* "Yep, I'm from Southern California. A little town not far from San Diego."
* "You live on Cornelis Street? Do you know so and so?"

Level Two: Bond Building

This is where you try and find out what things the two of you have in common other than the simple need to throw your bodies together. If you fish a little while, you can find out something about one of his special interests. Pick up on his mentioning of his dog, for example. If he says he has a golden retriever, maybe you can say you love that breed because you grew up with one. The sharing can grow deeper now, because you have two personal topics you can talk about: families and golden retrievers. Other good topics that inspire bond building are the three Cs; Collections, Cooking, and Cars. And in certain circles, don't overlook New Age issues. Sharing/talking about past lives, astrology, aromatherapy, or feng shui are all great topics that can catapult a conversation right out to the galaxies!

The Three Cs:

Collections

* ✽ "I have every album by Janis Joplin and Janis Ian. Two Janises from the same musical period, and they're not the least bit alike."
* ✽ "You say your sister collected Beanie Babies? Wow, I did, too."
* ✽ "I still have all my old copies of *Mad* magazine. I guess that's kind of embarrassing, but they're worth a lot now, too."

Cooking

* ✽ "I'd cook more except my kitchen's so small."
* ✽ "I never cook. My favorite entertainment is eating out."
* ✽ "You like huevos rancheros? Incredible! That's my signature dish!"
* ✽ "In my fantasy life, someone gives me a complete set of Caphalon."

Cars

* ✽ "I went to my senior prom in a yellow Corvette. My dress was dyed to match the car."
* ✽ "I've always had a thing for old Thunderbirds."
* ✽ "BMWs? My favorite wheels."

Level Three: The Serious Nitty-Gritty

Before you go any further getting to know this guy, there are usually a few things you need to find out before you can seriously consider going on a date with him. This is what is known as the Serious Nitty-Gritty. For example, if you could only get serious about a guy who shares your religious beliefs, this is the time to find out if you're on the same page here. Or if you could never envision yourself being with a guy who would never have a pet, you need to know how he feels about domestic animals. If you're the kind of woman who expects to spend most of the weekend with her boyfriend, you might want to know if his idea of nirvana is to spend all weekend in front of the TV watching the playoffs.

Try these questions on for size:

* "Are you a Christian?"
  If he says: "All religion is bogus to me," and you like to go to church on Sunday, you've got a problem.
* "Would you say you're more of a dog person or a cat person?"
  If he says: "If somebody gave me a cat, I'd kill it," change seats and leave this guy alone!
* "Describe for me your perfect Saturday."
  If he says: "Baby, I'd just like to devote my whole weekend to you," blush and give him your number.

Level Four: Real Intimacy

This is the place in the conversation where you share some secrets. Most people have to feel they're in a pretty safe place—emotionally and psychologically and physically—with another person to share intimate information about themselves. When you share a secret about yourself you leave yourself vulnerable. It's very hard to get men to Level Four on a first encounter. Usually it takes about five hours of deep conversation with a man to find out that he's, um . . . it's a secret. But once you know his secret, voilà, you have him (at least for the time being) in your hands.

If you're still hanging in there with him, proceed to Chapter 7.

GETTING HIS NUMBER

You want this guy's phone number? Here's how to ask for it.

* "Here's my number. What's yours?"
* "This is a good way to reach me. How do I reach you?"
* "I'm not big on e-mail. How do I reach you by phone?"
* "If I wanted to get in touch with you, what's the best way?"
* "Can I call you later?"
* "I need your digits."
* "How do you prefer to be contacted?"
* "What's the best way to reach you?"
* "Is that your cell number or your office number on your business card?"
* "What's a good time to call?"
* "I'm going to need your number."
* "Want to give me your number now?"

GREAT QUESTIONS BEYOND "WHAT'S YOUR SIGN?"

You've managed to learn his astrological sign. What do you say next to figure out what the stars have in store for you?

Aries: Ask the Ram, "Your sign is enthusiastic and courageous.

But you can be a daredevil, too. Tell me, how much risk are you comfortable with?"

Taurus: Ask the Bull, "I know you're very warm hearted, but are you the jealous type?"

Gemini: Ask the Twins, "Hmm, Geminis are known for being intellectual and witty and I can see you're all that. But are you a serious person? Or would you describe yourself as being more the opposite?"

Cancer: What to say to a Crab? "I've heard Cancers are real homebodies. Is your favorite activity curling up on the couch?"

Leo: What to say to a Lion? "Let me hear you roar."

Virgo: Say to a Virgin, "You're not really a virgin now, are you?"

Libra: What to say to the Scales? "Your sign is so romantic and charming. I bet you are the most amazing date."

Scorpio: What to say to the Scorpion? "Hmm. Your sign is so sexy. Are you a true Scorpio?"

Sagittarius: What to say to the Archer? "Uh-oh, I bet you're a real party animal!"

Capricorn: What to say to the Goat? "I love a man who is practical and prudent."

Aquarius: What to say to the Water Carrier? "Honesty and loyalty in a man are my number one priorities."

Pisces: Say to a Fish, "Your sign is known for its great imagination. Tell me some of your amazing dreams."

If you're still hanging in there with him, proceed to chapter 7.

Chapter Seven

Let's Kick This up a Notch

You've come a long way, baby, and now it's time to really strut your stuff. You've had lots of opps to practice your flirtation skills and it's time to stretch your flirt muscles even more and become bolder in your moves. In the scheme of your flirtation education, think of this chapter as flirtation finishing school. Here's where you learn to put the final polish on your moves—and get the guy! Now let's get out there and get your game on!

Most of the flirting you've been doing so far has been pretty harmless. It comes in handy for a brief flirtation and everyday life situations. But what happens when you're flirting with a guy and you decide you're really into him—and not just in a "let's share the bean dip" kind of way? Intention, of course, is everything. When you're ready to use your flirtation skills to move things to the next level, it's called flirting with a purpose.

A Little Word of Caution

The territory you're about to enter is another country, for sure. Be aware, especially if you're a very young woman and a fledgling flirter at best, this chapter might not be for you! You are about to enter a fairly grown-up world where girls and guys get it on with each other. Of course, lots of material here is still useful for girls with less experience or those who want to stay in the kiddie pool for a while longer, but realize that portions of this chapter are clearly not for everyone. Or, tuck this information away for later—it might not be right for you right now . . . but who knows what your flirting future holds in store for you!

Warning given—now let's proceed. There will definitely be occasions in your life when your flirting has a purpose *beyond* simple entertainment or passing the time while at a party. Maybe your intention or purpose is to get the object of your flirtation home in bed with you. Maybe you're hoping to forge a deeper relationship. Possibly you're trying to steer him to the altar. In any case, you get the drift: at this level, flirting is serious stuff!

When you're flirting with a purpose, the stakes are higher because you're taking a chance and there is a risk of rejection from the object of your flirtation. And, unlike most of your flirtations and flirtatious encounters, when you're flirting with a purpose, you actually care about the outcome.

However . . . before you take your show on the road, it's time to do a little review. In chapter 1 you found out what kind of flirt you are. In chapter 2 you mastered a few basic opening lines to break the ice, and learned some conversational gambits to help you talk about anything, anywhere. In chapter 3 you mastered how to use your voice like a body part and all about the fine art of whispering. In chapter 4 you became more adept at advancing a conversation and a bit about body language. In chapter 5 you got your first taste of taking your flirting skills out into the world, including the great wide world of the Internet, where you have myriad opportunities to flirt with people you'll never "see." In chapter 6 you learned about the different types of guys and their verbal styles, and how to deal with every kind of guy from the Mumbler to the Guy Who Can't Shut Up.

But before you plunge into using your best material on that guy you've been exchanging flirtatious lines with for the last four hours, take this quick assessment quiz to determine if this man is worthy of your going the whole nine yards.

He's Definitely Worth It If . . .

* You're not quite sure how you feel about him yet, but he is paying 100 percent rapt, devoted attention to you.
* He's so cute you'd swap spit with him no matter what he says or sounds like.
* He looks exactly like Brad Pitt.
* He looks exactly like Clive Owen.
* You want him. You need him. It has to be now.

He's Probably *Not* Worth It If . . .

* He's pretty hot—not exactly your type but you don't think you could date him unless he got a serious man make-over.
* You weren't that interested until you had another martini.
* You'd go home with him—but only to make your ex jealous.
* It's two A.M. and you're horny and he's the only man left standing.

He's *Definitely* Not Worth It If . . .

* Everything he says is smart and funny, but his breath is deplorable.
* He's yummier looking than Orlando Bloom but he's flat-on-his-butt drunk. Unless your dream is to have a gorgeous guy puke in your bed, forget about this one.
* You're having fun with him but he keeps calling you by the wrong name. Bad sign. Really bad sign.
* He returns from the men's room with his pants unzipped.

Have you decided? Does he rate? Is he worth your energy? If so, let's proceed to the next portion.

Puttin' the Moves on a Guy You Just Met

Sometimes you meet a guy and the electricity is instant! Or maybe it's the chemistry! Or the pheromones! Or whatever! You see he's not wearing a wedding ring and he sure is acting as if he hasn't been taken. You've decided to buy into the "I'm single" message he's putting out, but how do you let him know right off the bat that you're interested in getting to know him a lot better and not just for his mind? Deploy one of these bold-faced brazen badinages to ratchet up the intensity—pronto!

* "If you're going to kiss her hello, you'll have to kiss me too."
* "Something tells me we have a lot in common. How should we find out?"

* "Hmmm. You are just my type."
* "What are you doing later?"

To put a little muscle into your come-on overture, try combining a little body language into these different flirtstyle lines:

The Smooth Talker

The Move: Thrust out your chest.
The Words: "So, when are we going to get together?"

The Ditz

The Move: Bounce from one foot to the other.
The Words: "Omigosh, you're so cute. I definitely want you to call me!"

The Interrogator

The Move: Cock one hip.
The Words: "If you're not seeing anyone special, I think you should give me a call."

The Shy Girl

The Move: Lock your gaze only at the exact moment you're speaking the words.
The Words: "It would be nice to get to know you."

The Helper

The Move: Touch his forearm with a carefully manicured fingertip.

The Words: "Oh, that sounds so stressful. Do you think a little neck rub would help?"

The Comedienne

The Move: Look him up and down with an arched eyebrow. The Words: "Well, hello there."

Great Lines That Do the Work for You

If you've been chatting a guy up for longer than thirty minutes, then chances are you feel the conversation is going *very* well. So how do you let him know how you're feeling? There are certain words that telegraph a clear and strong signal to their recipient that the deliverer of the words is not beating around the bush regarding her intentions. Try using some of these hard-working lines to let your guy know *exactly* what you're saying.

* "I think you're really cute. Do you think I'm really cute?"
* "I'm just a sucker for a guy with [*insert correct eye color here*] eyes."
* "This is fun but I think I'd like to continue this conversation in a position that's horizontal."
* "Do you think we could go somewhere together and lie down?"
* "What are your plans, say, a half hour from now?"

Initiating a Hook-up

So you've been chatting with him all night and you're both sensing where things may be going (i.e., someplace private).

Everything in his body language (and yours!) is hollering "Let's get intimate," i.e., he's got his arm around your waist, he's sucking on your fingers, his hand is on your backside, you can't keep your hands off him. Your POD (Public Display of Affection) quotient is ratcheting off the charts. People are starting to look at you like they want to say, "Hey, you two. Get a motel room." Try on one of these playful lines that more or less invite him to take you home:

* At a *"Denim & Diamonds" type dance hall:* "Whatcha waitin' for, cowboy? A mating call?"

* At the *country club:* "Care to accompany me to my private accommodations?"

* At a *fund-raiser or swanky party:* "Wanna personally investigate the coat check room?"

* At *your cousin's wedding:* "Would you like to do what the bride and the groom will be doing tonight?"

* At *the bar in the hotel where your company is having their annual big pow-wow:* "Let's go upstairs and find out if this hotel has 'turn-down' service."

NURTURING YOUR INNER SEX KITTEN

Every woman, no matter her age or personality type, has it in her power to be a sex kitten. Or sex tiger! Sure, you may work in a job that requires you to squash down your sensuality, dress like a nun, or never allow a spicy word or phrase to pass your lips. But that doesn't mean you can't summon up some good, old-fashioned supervixen energy when you need it. And baby, to be a flirting expert, you need it!

Follow these tips to bringing out your inner virago (um, that means "sexy babe," "tart," "doll," "Chiquita").

* Wear stupendous underwear. Or don't wear underwear at all.

* Invest in a pair of supersexy jeans. If you can zip 'em up without inhaling, they're too big for you.

* Get a good haircut. It doesn't matter if your hair is short or long. What matters to guys is that your hair is soft and touchable, and that you don't have the kind of do where you're gonna go crazy if he runs his hands through it and messes it up.

* Learn how to apply eyeliner. Eye makeup is sexy, although you don't need to go overboard. For nighttime, wear more than you would during the day, and if you're a No Make-Up girl in general, get handy with an eye pencil and a mascara wand for going out at night. The idea is to draw attention to your eyes . . . so that when he looks into them, he really, deeply looks.

* Have one good red lipstick and don't be afraid to use it!

* Wear perfume. Splash some in your cleavage. If you don't have any cleavage, spritz some on your wrists, behind your ears—and even in your armpits. But not right after shaving!—Ouch!

* Own one pair of thong panties. You don't have to wear them, just own them.

* Put a satin pillow on your bed.

* Wear negligees.

* Make up a private name for yourself to go online with.

* Take tender care of your feet. Get pedicures.

* Be liberal with body moisturizing lotion. Rub shea butter into your skin every chance you get! Guys love soft, smooth, touchable skin!

* Keep nice sheets on your bed. The higher the thread count, the better.
* Take baths.
* Read a racy novel. One with lots of naughty parts.
* Rent an erotic movie. Anything by Candida Royalle's "Femme" features is good. (Go to www.candidaroyalle.com to preview her selection.)
* Consider buying a vibrator or Magic Wand. You won't regret it!
* Fantasize about that hunky guy whom you'd never date in a million years but wish you could. Go ahead, have fun with it! It's a fantasy!

Moving the Action into the Bedroom

The scene is set. You're in your apartment. You've lit some candles and turned the lights low. The music is just right, and the two of you are . . . getting to know one another a little better. But if you thought this is where your verbal flirtations end, you thought wrong! Just because you're fooling around a little bit doesn't mean that you should stop with the hot talk—especially if you feel ready to invite him to your bedroom. Unless things have reached that boiling point where words are irrelevant and the only sounds emanating from your mouth are utterly animalistic, you still need specialized dialogue to keep the vibe going. Try these phrases to urge him straight into your panties:

* "Let's hit the bedroom."
* "Follow me."
* "How about we get under the covers?"
* "Are you ready to make love to me now?"

* "I can't wait to find out what you taste like."
* "Your kisses are burning me up."
* "Come on and ravish me."
* "Put your finger right here."
* "Oh! You animal!"

Smooth Talker: "Follow me."

Ditzy: "Ouch, I think I'm getting rug burn. Could we move this somewhere else, doncha think?"

Interrogator: "How would you like to go into the bedroom?"

Shy Girl: "Um, the bed is more comfortable than the sofa."

Helper: "I think we'd be so much more comfortable between the sheets."

Comedienne: "You look cute with your pants all twisted around your knees, but don't you think it's time to lie down and get naked?"

Caught in the Act

Okay, the night has gone just right. You've been charming, witty, sexy, and entertaining all night long, and your hard work has paid off. You've now got your guy right where you want him—in the epicenter of all flirations—the bedroom. And make no mistake—what you say when you're intimate with a guy is just as important as making a first impression. Guys love it when women talk to them while they're "in the act." For one thing, it lets them know that what they're doing is appreciated and that they're doing a good job! The other great reason to keep on talking is that you can fuel your libido—and his—by using passionate words and cries. Here are some really good things to say in bed, especially when you're "caught in the act."

* *Speak some French.* Even if you don't know a word, just murmur or cry out the phrase *"C'est fou! Oh, c'est fou!"* (which is pronounced SAY-FOO). He probably won't know what you're saying either, but he'll know you're enjoying yourself!

* *Produce a running monologue about what you're feeling.* Giving vent to emotions like "I can't stand it, I'm about to scream" or "It's too much, don't stop now!"

* *Give directions.* You don't have to be a bully about it, but if there's something specific you need or want or a place on your body that has to be touched, tell the guy. Especially if it's only the first or second time you've been together! Unless you tell him that you really must have some attention paid to the back of your neck or you must be kissed on the lips during the climactic moments, how is he supposed to know? Give the guy a break and don't expect him to be a mind reader.

FIVE INCREDIBLY HOT THINGS TO SAY TO A MAN IN BED

These steamy sentences might sound straight out of a porno film—which is why men love hearing these words! Use these words to put your man in a state—a state of sexual agitation!

* "I'm definitely not a virgin."
* "I'm *very* orally fixated."

* "I'm afraid you're going to be too big for me but let's try it out."

Developing Meaningful Pillow Talk

Some things a woman can say to a man after sex are good—and others aren't. Did you ever wonder if the girl in that movie *Looking for Mr. Goodbar*, starring a much younger Diane Keaton and a much, much younger Richard Gere got murdered by her lover because she insulted his prowess?

In general, after you've been very intimate with someone, it's wise, first and foremost, to be generous and kind. If you've just had an orgasm, your bed partner has just given you a great gift. Thank him for the pleasure he's given you. A simple "Wow, that was great," or "You were awesome" will do. And if there was something he did that you really, really liked, tell him! Guys really enjoy knowing what worked with a particular woman—although they never like to hear what didn't. So praise the guy if he did something good. It's the best way to ensure that the next time you get it on with him, he'll do whatever it was again, and again!

Beyond stroking his ego (and guaranteeing that if it was twenty minutes of foreplay that got you hot and bothered, you'll soon get more of the same), plenty of things that guys and girls can talk about in bed will actually bring them closer. Emotionally closer, not just bodily closer.

If your guy seems open to it, try introducing one of these soul-baring topics. Just remember, these questions are kind of a Pandora's box and you may get more information than you asked for!

* "Were you always sexually precocious?"
* "When did you lose your virginity?"

* "The first time you had sex was it true love or just sex?"
* "Did you ever think about 'saving yourself' for marriage?"

Or . . . offer tidbits of information about yourself. A lot of times when a woman reveals some of her private story, it makes the guy want to share with her some of his. Some lines of conversation you might initiate might start like this:

* "I thought I'd be a virgin until I got married. Of course, I changed my mind when I was around nineteen."
* "The first time I did it, I thought, 'Omigod, this is weird,' but then I began to enjoy it."
* "If a girl has a boyfriend, I don't understand why she would want any sex toys. Do you?"

Just remember, once you get him to share, he's automatically more "involved" with you! Women like to believe that after a man has had sex with them that they've established a connection, but the truth is, the connection is only a connection of the flesh. Men really do take a more casual approach to sex than do women, which can lead to a great deal of misunderstanding in love's aftermath! If you want to be more than a hook-up or (ouch) booty call, more than a mere physical tie has to be established. Don't expect him to fall madly in love with you just because he had an orgasm—he won't. But if you hope to see him again and keep the vibe going, let him know that you're interested in getting to know who he is—and not just his body parts.

21 FOOLPROOF LINES YOU CAN'T LIVE WITHOUT

There are such things as foolproof lines. Here's twenty-one of the best ones!

1. "Gosh it's hot. I just might have to sleep naked."

2. "I'd love a drink."

3. "You're so funny."

4. "Why don't you bring over your laptop?"

5. "I think I'll just have to take some more clothes off."

6. "Get over here."

7. "Give me a taste of that."

8. "Other than you find me irresistible, is there a reason you're looking at me?"

9. "Married?"

10. "Well, hel-lo there."

11. "Surely you don't mean that."

12. "I love a man wearing . . . [whatever]"

13. "You have the most arresting eyes."

14. "I'll go wherever you're going."

15. "Your dog can sleep with me tonight."

16. "Shame? I have no shame."

17. "It takes a lot of guy to get me all hot and bothered."

18. "I was just leaving unless you can give me a reason to stay."

19. "I never sleep a wink without my teddy."

20. "Let's blow this joint."

21. "Oh, stop. Don't stop."

Morning-After Icebreakers

Even after the most fantastic night of passion, things can feel a bit awkward in the morning. Whether you want your bed-friend to stick around for breakfast or get him 10-4 out the door, make sure that your morning after, après-sex dialogue is easy and friendly, the kind of words that make him want to check in with you later and not just disappear into the cold.

There's a fine line between acting flippant or even indifferent and behaving like a desperate, clinging vine. There are some absolute no-no's for the morning after. Don't:

✳︎ Demand he write down all his phone and e-mail contacts and leave them on the pad by your night table.

✳︎ Make him promise to call you later.

✳︎ Hide an essential element of his personal belongings (his cell phone maybe?) so that he's forced to call you or come over later to see if it turned up.

✳︎ Start crying. Although tons of guys really dig damsels in distress, no guy alive enjoys exiting the apartment of a teary woman. So even if you are overwhelmed with romantic feelings following the best sex of your life, don't allow your hormones and your emotions to get the better of you! Save those tears for the shower!

There are some perky, positive things to say the morning after that will make you seem interested without seeming, well, *too* interested:

✳︎ "I had a great time."

✳︎ "Have a wonderful day at work!"

✳︎ "Thanks for bringing me home. I really enjoyed it!"

✳︎ "You know how to reach me."

✳︎ "Some coffee before you go? Although I don't have a spare travel cup."

If the morning after happens to be on a weekend or a holiday and rushing off to work isn't a valid reason to break up the beautiful moment, it's generally not a great idea to quiz the guy about what his plans are for later if he doesn't ask you first. The general rule of thumb to follow about male behavior is that if the guy wants to spend the day or even a part of the day with you after you just spent the night together, he *will* say something. On the other hand, if you ask him directly, he may not want to give you an answer, or he may give you a truthful answer that's unsatisfactory to you. For example, discovering that he'd rather catch up on his laundry than take you to brunch is unnecessarily demeaning.

And even so, it doesn't mean that's the end. It might just mean he's not ready to spend more time with you—and that he's got a scary amount of laundry. So avoid asking that question. He may very well still call you later after he's finished doing whatever it is he has to do. In this case an "Ask me no questions and I'll tell you no lies," policy is a good one to adopt. Besides, you might not want to be asking him a lot of questions because you don't want to have questions asked of yourself. *You* might be the one with other plans that don't include *him*.

Flirty Dating Dialogue to Keep Things Hot

Let's say that you've started dating. Depending on your definition, this could mean anything from a few casual dates together to your toothbrush's holding prime position in his medicine cabinet. To keep the sparks going, you can't drop your flirt guard now! To do so is to start to kill the relationship before it even really gets going. Don't rest on your laurels, to be sure. Now that you've gotten to know each other a little bit better, you don't have to work quite as hard to make a first impression, but you still have to work at holding his attention. That means keeping things exciting. The beginning stages of dating and relationships are chock full of opportunities for you to further hone your flirting skills. Try taking one or more of these little excursions to put a fine point on your ultimate sexy banter.

The Ultimate Threesome . . . You and Him and Some High-End Bathroom Fixtures

Go house and houseware shopping together. Even if you have no immediate intentions of living together, if you've been in the relationship for a few months, it's hot to go shopping for houses, apartments, condos, even time-shares. First of all, looking at all those bedrooms and bathrooms is infinitely sexy. Chances are, at this point in the relationship, whenever the two of you see a bed or a bathtub, you immediately picture yourselves naked in it.

But if going around to open houses on the weekends (and then running back to your apartment for a bout of hot sex) doesn't appeal to you or you suspect that doing such a thing will scare your great new guy off, take the emphasis down a notch and go on an excursion together to a home store. Again, it's that tiny whiff of domesticity that's so sexy and intoxicating, but the real deal is that these places evoke a primitive response in both of you—and that's hot! Try using any one of these great lines to keep your guy in a state of high arousal:

* "That shower looks big enough for two, don't you think?"
* "Hey, do you think my bedroom is large enough for a super-king-size bed!"
* "Wouldn't you like to wash my back in here?"
* "I wonder what it would be like to have our own Jacuzzi."
* "I've always wanted my own private undressing room."
* "You and me could get lost in here."
* "Have you ever done it in a bathtub?"
* "Wanna tumble my marble?"

In the Grocery Store

If food shopping is your least favorite chore next to taking out the garbage, get your mate to tag along the next time you have to handle a grocery cart. Convince him to do the bagging by alluding to all the fun things you have in mind to do with the grape jelly if only he can get you out of that line faster. While you're actually in the store, entertain your honey using any one of these great lines:

* *By the dairy case:* "Let's get this premium unsalted imported butter. I know it's expensive, but I've got another job for it besides buttering up your toast."
* *In the meat aisle :* "Aren't you glad I'm into beef?"
* *Over by the condiments:* "Hmm. What else do you think we could do with this jar of maraschino cherries?"
* *In frozen foods:* "Let's skip the ice cream and go directly to the chocolate sauce. I can't wait to go home and get sticky."

Chapter Eight

A Flirtspeak Farewell

Now that you've reached the end of this book and you're a first-class flirt, let's take a moment to review what you've learned. For starters, you know what your natural flirting style is—comic, sincere, inquisitive, smooth, or a bit silly. You also know that you don't have to stick to one style . . . that when the occasion arises for you to shift flirting gears, you can easily segue from being a Comedienne, to say, a Helper. You also know how to size up different kinds of guys, and know what lines might work best on them!

You've also gained confidence to speak in groups and to approach guys you've never spoken to before, and know what to say to keep the ball rolling after the first opening lines. You have picked up a bit of body language to augment your words. For example, now you know that anytime a woman lays even a finger on a man, it sets off a spark of electricity! And now you have the words in your arsenal of feminine tools of the flirting trade to keep that first spark going and turn it into a true flame.

Just because you've made it this far doesn't mean that your flirting journey is over. Far from it! This book has given you the skills (and even the actual words to use to deploy those skills) to help you when you're out flirting. Whom you're flirting with and why are certainly matters of personal preference. You may believe it's just not worth your time to flirt with guys whom you don't think you could seriously become interested in. And that's fine. Or you could be the type of woman who flirts with lots of guys—available and not so available!—just to keep your skill level up so that you're ready to play once you find *the* guy. Or you may be the kind of woman who enjoys flirting for flirting's sake—because it makes you feel good, makes the person you're flirting with feel good, and it's a pleasant way sometimes to pass the time of day.

Remember that a great deal of good flirting is not about finding and mating with the perfect man. It's also fun to flirt with men you'll never meet again (like that guy who sat next to you on a plane) or with a baby (babies are so naturally flirtatious that it's almost impossible to resist their innocent flirtatiousness) or with another woman (gasp!) in order to attract the attention of a man. There are as many reasons for flirting as there are people in the universe. It's all up to you how you want to use your newfound skills and practice your art.

Is flirting an art? Some say yes, others not. One thing is for certain. Flirting certainly makes life more interesting. So go out there and flirt! Take the knowledge you have gleaned from this book and pass it on to other women. You never know what good things may come your way because of it!

THE FLIRTSPEAK GLOSSARY

Many flirtatious expressions have been used throughout this book to help guide you how to act, speak, and behave. Because these words and phrases may not be part of your normal conversational vernacular, this glossary is meant to act as a dictionary to help you understand what these words mean.

ABCs of Flirting: Approach, Behavior, and Control

Advancing the communication: The statement or question that takes the initial icebreaker opening comment to the next level of communication

Babbling: A nervous verbal tic or habit that keep a person talking long after he or she should have stopped

Babbling Band-Aids: Quick fixes to banish babbling for good

Body language: A physical form of communication in which the body, not the mouth, does the talking

Booty language: A very specialized form of communication in which all body language and verbal language points toward getting the two of you sexually intimate

Clinger: A guy who seems promising at the beginning of the night, but he latches on and won't let go

Conversation starter: An icebreaking gambit used to get two people talking

Conversation stopper: Any word or phrase or sentence that stops all communication cold

Crush at first sight: A die-hard flirter's version of love at first sight

Deal breakers: Any habits a guy has that immediately cancel out the possibility of a relationship, no matter how promising he may seem

Double entendre: A word or phrase that has a double meaning, one of which may be risqué

E-flirting: Flirting via e-mail, IM, or any other electronic means

Fledgling flirter: A person who is just getting started in her flirtation education

Flirt around: Flirting in a group or with more than one person at a time with no particular or set-in-stone objective

Flirtation education: The advancement or furthering of flirtatious skills and techniques

Flirtation situation: Any situation in which a flirtation may occur

Flirting like you mean it: Flirting with the specific goal of getting a guy to ask you out

Flirtstick: Control of the flirtation situation. "You're holding the flirtstick" means that you're in control.

Flirt object: The person to whom all flirting efforts are directed even temporarily

Flirtspeak: The sexy language of flirtation

Flirtspeak method: Any of the flirtation tactics set forth in this book

Flirting type: Your flirting personality, as defined in chapter 1

Flirttress: A cross between flirt and seductress; a woman who excels at the art of flirtatious seduction.

Four Levels of Intimacy: Four levels of communicating and sharing information that enhance connection and intimacy

Grunter: A human being who eschews most normal forms of communication to engage in primitive sounds, i.e. grunts

Guy speak: the secret language (often indecipherable) of males

Harmless flirting: Flirting to pass the time of day, such as in line at the bank or coffee shop

Nitty gritty: The serious details about a guy that will determine whether you want to take the flirtation to the next level

Object of your flirtation: Any guy with whom you've decided to start up a flirtation

One Two Punch: A technique of delivering one great flirtatious line and then quickly following it up with another before the flirt object has time to catch his breath

Only foolin': Lighthearted flirting for fun, not with serious intention

Parrying: A verbal technique used to shift subjects or help evade or avoid answering a question one prefers not to answer or to take the conversation in a direction that is disadvantageous to your goals

Three C's: Three conversational topics that can inspire bond building in a flirtation situation. The three Cs are: Collections, Cooking, and Cars

Ultimate flirting: Flirting with serious intent, as in "I wanna go home with this guy."

Verbal tickle: A spoken word or phrase that immediately conjures up an atmosphere of flirtatiousness.

Wingman: a traveling, bar-hopping, party-going buddy who helps you talk with and connect with possible Flirt objects.

ACKNOWLEDGMENTS

In making *Flirtspeak* possible I would first like to thank my agent, June Clark, who coached me through the proposal and who brokered the deal. I'd also like to thank the very talented, patient, thoughtful, outstanding Danielle Chiotti, my editor, who took all my sometimes uncouth raw material and made sense of it. Thanks, Danielle! You did an amazing job! A big thanks, too, goes to Kristen Hayes, the designer of the cover, and the sales force, Helen Dressner, David Lappin, Karen Fink, and Doug Mendini, as well as all the other dedicated people at Citadel who made *Flirtspeak* the outstanding package that it is.

For all their help and encouragement and especially for agreeing to share their best flirting tips with me, I'd like to thank my young friends at the barn, the great group of flirty girls I ride horses with. Johanna, Kristin, and Elizabeth, thank you so much! And a very special thanks to my trainer, Alex Hamer, my guiding light.

I'd also like to thank my husband, "Mr. Saxophone," R. J. Marx, who has put up with my outrageous flirting for many years. And my son, Sam, a natural-born flirt with the flirt gene in his genes. Last but not least, I'd like to thank my special equine companions, the beautiful white ponies Sidney and Trifle, for daily instructing me in equine/human flirtatious relations. Boys, I could not have written this book without you!

La série XIII a été créée par WILLIAM VANCE et JEAN VAN HAMME

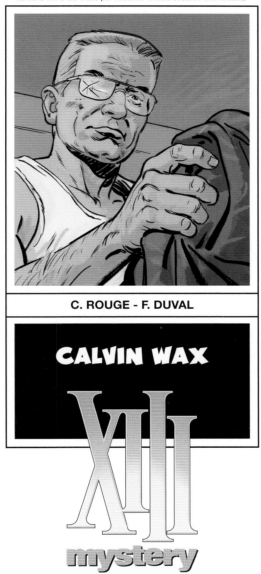

C. ROUGE - F. DUVAL

CALVIN WAX

XIII
mystery

Collection dirigée par Jean Van Hamme

Couleurs : Alexandre Boucq & Corentin Rouge

DARGAUD
BENELUX

*Merci à Yves et à Jean pour leur patience, à Éric Corbeyran pour sa disponibilité,
à Colin Wilson et à Frank Giroud pour leur interactivité.*

F. Duval

Logo : William Vance

www.dargaud.com

ABC NEWS VIRGINIE, IL EST 7 HEURES, VOICI VOTRE FLASH D'INFORMATION.

LE PRÉSIDENT SHERIDAN ÉTAIT HIER SOIR À RICHMOND OÙ IL A PRONONCÉ UN DISCOURS TRÈS ATTENDU SUR SA POLITIQUE SOCIALE.

À MI-MANDAT, LE PRÉSIDENT, DONT LA COTE DE POPULARITÉ EST AU BEAU FIXE, S'EST PLUS QUE JAMAIS AFFIRMÉ COMME LE DÉFENSEUR DES DROITS CIVIQUES ET DES SERVICES PUBLICS, FAISANT DE L'ÉCOLE ET DE L'HÔPITAL SES PRIORITÉS POUR LE PROCHAIN BUDGET FÉDÉRAL.

ON PEUT DIRE QU'IL A LANCÉ HIER SOIR LES BASES DE LA CAMPAGNE POUR SA RÉÉLECTION DANS DEUX ANS.

ÉTEINS-MOI CE TÉLÉVISEUR, PAUL, JE NE SUPPORTE PLUS LE BARATIN COMMUNISTE DE CES TRAÎTRES CORROMPUS.

BIEN, MONSIEUR WAX.

3

CES JOURNALISTES SONT PIRES QUE LES NÈGRES ET LES JUIFS PARCE QU'ILS SONT AUX ORDRES DES POLITICARDS DÉMOCRATES ET RÉPUBLICAINS!

C'EST TERMINÉ, BILLY BOY?

OUAIS, CALVIN.

HEUREUSEMENT, DES PATRIOTES ONT ACCEPTÉ DE SE LEVER POUR INSTAURER DANS CE PAYS LE RÉGIME QUI RENDRA SA SUPRÉMATIE À LA RACE BLANCHE!

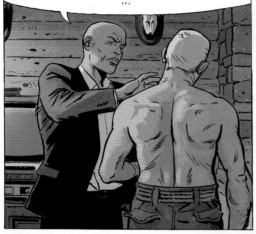

LES NÈGRES MÉRITENT DE POURRIR COMME DES FRUITS AU BOUT D'UNE CORDE, BIEN ENTENDU, MAIS POUR MENER VOTRE ACTION, CES TATOUAGES SONT-ILS BIEN NÉCESSAIRES? JE VEUX DIRE: SI QUELQU'UN DÉJOUAIT LE COMPLOT, IL SERAIT TRÈS SIMPLE DE VOUS IDENTIFIER...

DEPUIS LES LÉGIONS ROMAINES, LE TATOUAGE A POUR LE SOLDAT UN SENS QUI VA AU-DELÀ DE L'ENGAGEMENT! C'EST UNE PROTECTION. CHEZ LES SS., IL ÉTAIT APPELÉ «KAINSMAL», LA MARQUE DE CAÏN...

LA CONJURATION DES XX VA CHANGER LE COURS DE L'HISTOIRE. CES MARQUES INDÉLÉBILES INTERDISENT À SES MEMBRES TOUTE TENTATION DE RECUL... IL N'Y AURA AUCUNE RÉDEMPTION POSSIBLE.

JE COMPRENDS, MONSIEUR. AU FAIT... AVEZ-VOUS VISIONNÉ LA VIDÉO?

JE L'AI VUE. CE FILM NE SUFFIRA PAS À NOUS DÉBARRASSER DU PRÉSIDENT DES ÉTATS-UNIS—NOTRE PLAN IMPLIQUE UNE MORT VIOLENTE—MAIS IL SERVIRA LA CAUSE...

VOUS AVEZ FAIT DU BON TRAVAIL, PAUL.

JE M'ATTENDAIS À CE QUE CE SOIT VOUS, LE NUMÉRO I !

C'EST UN TITRE QUE JE RÉSERVE AU DERNIER ÉLÉMENT QUE NOUS ALLONS RECRUTER, CE N'EST PLUS QU'UNE QUESTION DE JOURS, LES SHERIDAN SONT EXTRÊMEMENT POPULAIRES, SEUL CAÏN POURRA FAIRE OUBLIER ABEL AU PEUPLE... MÊME SI, DANS NOTRE CAS, C'EST L'AÎNÉ QUI VA MOURIR.

WALLY SHERIDAN ! WALLY EST LE NUMÉRO I ! C'EST DONC ABEL QUI PORTERA LA MARQUE DE CAÏN.

À UN DÉTAIL PRÈS ...

... IL L'IGNORE ENCORE !

PAW

WAX ! TOUJOURS AUSSI PONCTUEL ! BIENVENUE, MON VIEUX !

MERCI DE M'ACCORDER CE RENDEZ-VOUS, SÉNATEUR SHERIDAN !

JE ME SUIS DIT QU'ICI, ON SERAIT TRANQUILLES, PAS DE DOMESTIQUES, PAS DE CONSEILLERS, PAS DE GARDES DU CORPS...

JE SUIS OFFICIELLEMENT EN WEEK-END EN GÉORGIE À LA PÊCHE EN TORRENT AVEC DES ANCIENS DE HARVARD !

J'IGNORAIS L'EXISTENCE DE CETTE GARÇONNIÈRE !

NORMAL, TU ES ICI CHEZ UNE AMIE.... JE COMPTE SUR TA LÉGENDAIRE DISCRÉTION, BIEN ENTENDU.

CALVIN ! ...

TU CONNAIS FORCÉMENT JULIA BROOKS !

JULIA CHÉRIE, JE TE PRÉSENTE CALVIN WAX, CONSEILLER DU VICE-PRÉSIDENT GALBRAIN.

J'AI VU LA PLUPART DE VOS FILMS, MISS. J'AVOUE AVOIR PARTICULIÈREMENT APPRÉCIÉ « RETOUR À SAIGON ».

CETTE BOUSE PSEUDO-PATRIOTIQUE? T'AS AIMÉ ÇA, CALVIN ?... T'ES PAS TROP DIFFICILE, DIS-MOI! MÊME MES NICHONS N'ÉTAIENT PAS À LA HAUTEUR!

ALLEZ, JE T'OFFRE UN VERRE À LA SANTÉ DES VÉTÉRANS.

BLOODY MARY ? C'EST TOUT CE QUE J'AI !

LE DÉJEUNER VOUS ATTEND AU SOLEIL SUR LA TERRASSE DE LA PISCINE, SI LE TRAITEUR L'A DÉPOSÉ OÙ JE LE LUI AI DIT, M'ATTENDEZ PAS, J'AI PAS FAIM.

À VOS FUTURS SUCCÈS, MISS BROOKS !

ON DESCEND JUSQU'AUX BERGES DU POTOMAC ?

AVEC PLAISIR, WALLY.

QUEL MAGNIFIQUE JARDIN ! COMMENT SE CROIRE À 15 MINUTES DO CENTRE DE WASHINGTON DC,?!

OUI, C'EST MAGIQUE. TU SAIS QUE LES LYNX RÔDENT ET CHASSENT ENCORE DANS CES BOIS À LA TOMBÉE DE LA NUIT ?

CETTE FILLE EST INCONTRÔLABLE, WALLY ! TU CONNAIS SA RÉPUTATION. IL Y A QUELQUES ANNÉES ELLE ALTERNAIT FILMS ET CURES DE DÉSINTOX. AUJOURD'HUI, ELLE N'EST MÊME PLUS CAPABLE D'ARRIVER À L'HEURE CHEZ SON DEALER.

JE SUIS AMOUREUX D'ELLE, CALVIN ! JE VAIS L'AIDER À SE SORTIR DE SES ADDICTIONS. ELLE A UN TAS DE PROJETS, ICI, SUR LA CÔTE EST, TU SAIS !

SI J'EN CROIS LA PRESSE, ELLE A SURTOUT DE GROS SOUCIS FINANCIERS EN CALIFORNIE ! SA SOCIÉTÉ DE PRODUCTION À HOLLYWOOD A FAIT FAILLITE... QUI TE L'A PRÉSENTÉE ?

JE L'AI RENCONTRÉE CHEZ ANDY WARHOL, ELLE VENAIT DE ROMPRE AVEC UN DE CES PETITS JUNKIES QUI HANTENT LES SOIRÉES « HYPE » DE MANHATTAN !

WARHOL, J'AI SUR LUI UN DOSSIER HAUT COMME L'IMMEUBLE QUI ABRITE SA FACTORY !

TU SAIS QUE LE 33 UNION SQUARE WEST ABRITE AUSSI LA PERMANENCE DU PARTI COMMUNISTE AMÉRICAIN ?

DE QUOI VOULAIS-TU ME PARLER, CALVIN ?

8

DE TON FRÈRE. JE NE LE CROISE QUASIMENT PLUS DEPUIS QU'IL EST DEVENU PRÉSIDENT. JE DOIS DIRE QUE LA DÉLICIEUSE CORDULA Y EST POUR BEAUCOUP.

MA BELLE-SOEUR EXÉCUTE LES CONSIGNES DU PRÉSIDENT. RIEN DE PLUS.

SI TU AVAIS CESSÉ DE DÉFENDRE BÉNÉVOLEMENT TOUS LES PSYCHOPATHES D'AMÉRIQUE, COMME CE BOUCHER DE L'ALABAMA, OU BIEN DE GÉRER EN SOUS-MAIN LES INTÉRÊTS DE SONNY BARGER ET DE SES HELLS ANGELS, OU PIRE, DE CES ENFOIRÉS EN CAGOULE DU KLAN MON FRÈRE NE T'AURAIT SANS DOUTE PAS AIGUILLÉ VERS LE CABINET DU VICE-PRÉSIDENT GALBRAIN ! TU LE SAIS, CALVIN...

CES TUEURS DE RACE BLANCHE ME FASCINENT, WALLY, ET PUIS, SELON LA CONSTITUTION, ILS ONT DROIT À UN AVOCAT, N'EST-CE PAS ?

TU SAIS, TON FRÈRE N'A PAS TOUJOURS EU DE SCRUPULES À FRÉQUENTER LES HELLS ANGELS. JE VAIS TE FAIRE UNE CONFIDENCE SUR NOTRE PREMIÈRE RENCONTRE.

JE CONNAIS L'HISTOIRE : TU FAISAIS TON DROIT À L'UNIVERSITÉ DE LOS ANGELES, MON FRÈRE VENAIT DE HARVARD ET FAISAIT UN STAGE DE TERRAIN À DOWNTOWN L.A.

VOUS VOUS ÊTES CONNUS LORS D'UN DÉBAT QUI A TOURNÉ AU CONCOURS DE BOISSON, À MOINS QUE CE NE SOIT L'INVERSE.

ÇA, C'EST CE QU'ON A TOUJOURS RACONTÉ, MAIS LA VÉRITÉ EST TOUT AUTRE...

..LE JOUR OÙ J'AI CONNU TON FRÈRE, AVEC MES AMIS, NOUS AVONS COMMENCÉ PAR LUI SAUVER LA VIE !

AVANT D'ÉPOUSER UNE CARRIÈRE
POLITIQUE ET DE RÉALISER LES
RÊVES DE VOTRE PÈRE ET DU
CLAN SHERIDAN, TON FRÈRE
AVAIT TENU À OBSERVER LA
POPULATION LA PLUS DÉMUNIE
DU PAYS. DÉJÀ SA SATANÉE
FIBRE SOCIALE QUI LE HANTAIT,
N'EST-CE PAS ? IL TRAVAILLAIT
DONC POUR UNE ASSOCIATION
DE PRÉVENTION MÉDICALE
DANS LE QUARTIER DE WATTS,
UN DES PLUS PAUVRES DE
LOS ANGELES, RONGÉ PAR LE
TRAFIC DE DROGUE ET LA
GUERRE DES GANGS.

C'ÉTAIT EN 1965. EN AOÛT, LES
FAMEUSES ÉMEUTES ONT ÉCLATÉ...

DES JOURS ET DES NUITS DE BATAILLES
DE RUE, DE PILLAGES ET D'INCENDIES...

DES DEALERS NÈGRES QUI DIRIGEAIENT
LE QUARTIER EN PROFITAIENT POUR
ÉLOIGNER OU ÉLIMINER DES
GÊNEURS COMME TON FRÈRE.

LAISSEZ-MOI FAIRE MON JOB, JE N'AI RIEN
CONTRE VOUS !

JE TE L'AI
DÉJÀ DIT,
SHERIDAN ! ON
N'AIME PAS LES
ASSISTANTS
SOCIAUX PAR
ICI !

VOUS ME
CONNAISSEZ, JE
TRAVAILLE ICI
!

SURTOUT LES BLANCS-BECS
QUI VIENNENT DE LA CÔTE
EST
!

10

LAISSE CE CITOYEN AMÉRICAIN, NEGRO!

MOI, J'ÉTAIS VENU M'ENGAGER DANS LES ÉMEUTES AVEC QUELQUES ANGES DE MES AMIS, DES GARS QUI AVAIENT DE L'EXPÉRIENCE POUR AVOIR DÉJÀ AFFRONTÉ LES MANIFESTANTS ANTI-GUERRE DU VIÊTNAM À BERKELEY...

BREF, TON FRÈRE ALLAIT SE FAIRE REFROIDIR PAR DES NÈGRES, NOUS, ON ÉTAIT LÀ POUR EN CASSER. ALORS ON A TOUT DE SUITE FAIT AFFAIRE...

LE TOUT-PUISSANT ÉTAIT AVEC VOUS AUJOURD'HUI, MON VIEUX, CETTE RACAILLE ALLAIT VOUS TUER.

ENCORE SOUS LE CHOC, TON FRÈRE NOUS A EXPLIQUÉ DE FAÇON ASSEZ CONFUSE QU'IL ESPÉRAIT UN JOUR PORTER POLITIQUEMENT UN GRAND PROGRAMME SOCIAL POUR TOUS LES QUARTIERS DIFFICILES... J'AI TOUT DE SUITE SENTI GERMER LA MAUVAISE GRAINE DÉMOCRATE.

MOI, J'ÉTUDIE LE DROIT ET JE N'AIME PAS LES DÉMOCRATES DANS TON GENRE, MAIS ENCORE MOINS LES RÉPUBLICAINS QUI NE SONT QUE DES FAUX DURS.

TOUS CES FÉDÉRALISTES SONT INCAPABLES DE TENIR TÊTE AUX COMMUNISTES AU VIÊTNAM! ILS VONT MENER LE PAYS À SA PERTE! L'AMÉRIQUE DOIT SORTIR DE SON BIPARTISME TRADITIONNEL, SEUL UN RÉGIME AUTORITAIRE LUI PERMETTRA DE RÉSISTER AUX ROUGES!

SI VOUS VOULEZ SURVIVRE DANS CE QUARTIER, FAUDRA REVENIR AVEC VOTRE ÉPÉE ET LAISSER VOTRE MÉDAILLE D'ARGENT CHEZ VOUS, WILLIAM SHERIDAN!

?!!

MAIS BIEN SÛR!

SONNY A RAISON! VOUS ÊTES CE SHERIDAN QUI A GAGNÉ UNE MÉDAILLE À L'ÉPÉE AUX JEUX OLYMPIQUES!

EN FLEURET PAR ÉQUIPES!

ON TE DÉPOSE QUELQUE PART, CHAMPION?

IL M'A INVITÉ À DÎNER POUR ME REMERCIER. NOUS SOMMES DEVENUS BONS AMIS. TON FRÈRE ÉTAIT DÉJÀ CONVAINCU QU'UN HOMME POLITIQUE DOIT SAVOIR S'ENTOURER ET QU'IL EST NÉCESSAIRE D'AVOIR SON EXACT CONTRAIRE DANS SON PREMIER CERCLE. MOI, JE L'AI PRIS POUR UN JEUNE LOUP AUX DENTS DE LAIT, QUI SE LAISSERAIT MANIPULER POUR ACCÉDER PLUS VITE AU POUVOIR.

RIING

ALLÔ?

LE PRÉSIDENT SHERIDAN EST DEVENU UNE MENACE POUR NOTRE CIVILISATION, WALLY.

SA POLITIQUE SOCIALE DÉSASTREUSE EST EN TRAIN DE RUINER LE PAYS, TOUT EN ASSISTANT LA LIE DE LA NATION, MAIS IL Y A PIRE...

...CUBA!

QUOI, CUBA?

TON FRÈRE S'EST FICHU EN TÊTE DE NÉGOCIER LA PAIX AVEC CASTRO! IL VEUT LEVER L'EMBARGO! ÇA SIGNIFIE QU'IL AUTORISERA LE COMMERCE AVEC LES COMMUNISTES!!! AUTANT LEUR DONNER LES CLEFS DU PENTAGONE ET DE LA MAISON-BLANCHE!

IL N'ANNONCERA RIEN AVANT LES ÉLECTIONS, MAIS EN CAS DE SECOND MANDAT, IL PASSERA À L'ACTE.

OOOOONNNN

OOOONNNN

?

?!

ATTENTION, WALLY, TON FRÈRE SAIT QUE TU REFUSES DE TRAITER AVEC LES COMMUNISTES, ALORS IL VA TE METTRE AU PLACARD. POUR ÇA, IL EST EN TRAIN DE FACILITER LA VIE À UN CANDIDAT RÉPUBLICAIN AFIN QU'IL TE BATTE DANS LE DELAWARE AUX PROCHAINES SÉNATORIALES.

TU DOIS RÉAGIR, ET VITE!

COMMENT SAIS-TU TOUT ÇA, CALVIN?

NNOOOONNNN

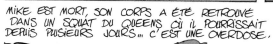

CHÉRIE! QU'EST-CE QUI SE PASSE ?

MIKE EST MORT, SON CORPS A ÉTÉ RETROUVÉ DANS UN SQUAT DU QUEENS OÙ IL POURRISSAIT DEPUIS PLUSIEURS JOURS... C'EST UNE OVERDOSE.

SI J'ÉTAIS RESTÉE AVEC LUI, IL SERAIT TOUJOURS EN VIE, TU M'ENTENDS ?!

ALLONS, MISS, CALMEZ-VOUS!

JE VEUX ALLER À NEW YORK, MAINTENANT! LÂCHEZ-MOI!

QUI VOUS PERMET DE...?

IL A RAISON, WALLY! ELLE FAIT UNE CRISE D'HYSTÉRIE. AVEC TOUTE LA COKE QU'ELLE A DANS LE NEZ, C'EST PAS ÉTONNANT!

TU DEVRAIS PARTIR, WALLY, JE VAIS M'OCCUPER DE TOUT.

HORS DE QUESTION!

14

LE CALMANT VA FAIRE EFFET D'ICI QUELQUES MINUTES. REPOSE-TOI, CHÉRIE... DEMAIN MATIN, NOUS PARTIRONS POUR NEW YORK, JE TE LE PROMETS.

T'ES UN AMOUR, WALLY.

NE VA PAS À NEW YORK AVEC ELLE, WALLY, J'AI UN MAUVAIS PRESSENTIMENT. TON ÉPOUSE NE SUPPORTERAIT PAS QUE TU SOIS MÊLÉ À UN NOUVEAU SCANDALE... VIENS CHEZ MOI, NOUS IRONS À LA CHASSE PENDANT QUE PAUL VEILLERA SUR JULIA !

TU SAIS QUE JE SUIS PRUDENT, CALVIN. ALLEZ, ON SE VOIT LUNDI ! DÉJEUNER CHEZ GEORGIO, C'EST MOI QUI INVITE. TU ME DIRAS CE QUE MON CHARMANT FRÈRE TRAME EXACTEMENT CONTRE MOI POUR CES ÉLECTIONS.

J'AI UN DÎNER DE TRAVAIL À WASHINGTON CE SOIR. JE NE PARTIRAI POUR LE SUD QUE DEMAIN, SI TU CHANGES D'AVIS, APPELLE MON DÉPARTEMENT DE D.C., PAUL PASSERA TE PRENDRE.

TU SAIS QUE TU PEUX COMPTER SUR MOI QUOI QU'IL ARRIVE, N'EST-CE PAS ?

TU ES UN AMI, CALVIN.

LA FENÊTRE DE TIR EST OUVERTE.

BIEN REÇU.

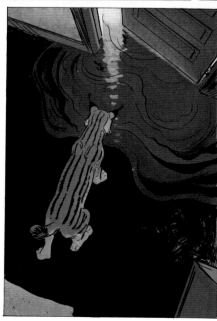

"' S'IL PRÉVIENT LES FLICS DU COMTÉ ?

ET S'IL NE NOUS TÉLÉPHONE PAS ?...'

IL NE LE FERA PAS, LES SHERIDAN NE TÉLÉPHONENT JAMAIS AUX FLICS QUAND ILS ONT UN PROBLÈME !

BILLY BOY EST ENCORE DANS LE JARDIN ET ÉCOUTE LA LIGNE DE LA MAISON. IL LA COUPERA SI NÉCESSAIRE....

"' MAIS ÇA N'ARRIVERA PAS.

DKII..

LAISSONS SONNER TROIS FOIS !

DRÍNG

CALVIN WAX, J'ÉCOUTE.

18

IL DEVAIT ÊTRE 23 HEURES, JULIA DORMAIT ENFIN...

UN BRUIT M'A ATTIRÉ VERS L'EXTÉRIEUR. J'AI PENSÉ À CES FOUTUES BESTIOLES QUI RÔDENT LA NUIT POUR FAIRE LES POUBELLES.

À PEINE SORTI, J'AI DÛ PRENDRE UN VIOLENT COUP SUR LA TÊTE, PARCE QUE JE NE ME SOUVIENS DE RIEN. J'AI ENCORE UN MAL DE CHIEN.

VILAINE BOSSE AU SOMMET DU CRÂNE, EN EFFET, TU N'AS PAS PU TE FAIRE ÇA EN TOMBANT !...

JE ME SUIS RÉVEILLÉ DANS CE CANAPÉ.

IL Y AVAIT UN LYNX DANS LA MAISON... L'ODEUR DU SANG L'A ATTIRÉ.

C'EST UN MEURTRE, CALVIN !!!

19

UN MEURTRE DÉGUISÉ EN SUICIDE... MAIS QUI POUVAIT LUI EN VOULOIR ? TOUT LE MONDE AIME JULIA !

MMH...

"...NE TE FAIS PAS D'ILLUSIONS, SI LES FLICS DÉBARQUENT, SOIT ILS CONCLUERONT AU SUICIDE, SOIT TU SERAS LE PRINCIPAL SUSPECT, WALLY ! DANS LES DEUX CAS, TU SERAS MÊLÉ À UN TERRIBLE SCANDALE, IL FAUT QUE TU PENSES À TA FEMME, À TA FAMILLE..."

QUELQU'UN SAVAIT-IL QUE TU PASSAIS LE WEEK-END ICI ?

NON.

RÉFLÉCHIS BIEN : EST-CE QUE QUELQU'UN D'AUTRE QUE PAUL ET MOI T'A VU ICI DEPUIS TON ARRIVÉE ?

LE TRAITEUR EST PASSÉ... J'ÉTAIS EN HAUT, IL N'A PAS PU ME VOIR.

BIEN, IL FAUT QUE TU TE SOUVIENNES DU MOINDRE ENDROIT DE CETTE MAISON OÙ TU AS CULBUTÉ CETTE FILLE, PARCE QUE, VU SA NOTORIÉTÉ, FAIS-MOI CONFIANCE, LES FLICS VONT TOUT PASSER AU CRIBLE.

JE VEUX SAVOIR QUI L'A TUÉE, CALVIN !... JE VEUX LE SAVOIR ET PENDRE MOI-MÊME CE FILS DE PUTE !!!

WALLY ! JE DOIS TE MONTRER QUELQUE CHOSE, CHEZ MOI, EN VIRGINIE... C'EST À 4 HEURES DE ROUTE. PAUL S'OCCUPERA DE RAMENER TA VOITURE QUAND IL AURA FINI LE NETTOYAGE DE LA MAISON.

QU'AS-TU À ME MONTRER, CALVIN ? CELA A-T-IL UN RAPPORT AVEC LA MORT DE JULIA ?

C'EST UN DOCUMENT IMPORTANT QUI CONCERNE PRINCIPALEMENT TON FRÈRE.

TU SAIS... PARFOIS JE ME DEMANDE S'IL EST RESTÉ LA FINE LAME QU'IL ÉTAIT AUTREFOIS...

FLEXION...

"AMORCE DU COUP, TRÈS BIEN!

ATTENTION AU TEMPO DU BRAS!

PARADE!

RÉPONSE!

PLEIN CŒUR...

...TU ES MORT, CALVIN WAX!

FORCER L'ADVERSAIRE À ATTAQUER POUR LE POUSSER À LA FAUTE! C'EST UNE STRATÉGIE SOUVENT PAYANTE AU FLEURET COMME EN POLITIQUE!

LA TAILLE ET LA MOBILITÉ DE CERTAINS GIBIERS M'OBLIGENT À GARDER UNE PRÉFÉRENCE POUR L'ARC DE CHASSE ET LE GROS CALIBRE.

IL FAUT POURTANT PARFOIS SAVOIR COMBATTRE À FLEURET MOUCHETÉ, CALVIN !

JE SAIS, EN TANT QU'AVOCAT, IL M'ARRIVE DE JOUER À CES PETITS JEUX !

C'EST JUSTEMENT À L'AVOCAT QUE JE VOULAIS PARLER, AUTANT QU'À L'AMI.

JE VAIS TENTER DE ME FAIRE ÉLIRE À LA CHAMBRE DES REPRÉSENTANTS.

CE N'EST QU'UNE DEMI-SURPRISE, WILLIAM !

JE SERAI DÉPUTÉ PENDANT QUELQUES ANNÉES, LE TEMPS DE ME FAIRE UN NOM AU SEIN DU PARTI DÉMOCRATE...

...PUIS CE SERA LA CONQUÊTE DU SÉNAT, ET ENFIN CELLE DU MANDAT SUPRÊME,

PRÉSIDENT ! WILLIAM SHERIDAN, PRÉSIDENT DES ÉTATS-UNIS D'AMÉRIQUE !...

TU SAIS QUE JE NE VOTERAI PAS FORCÉMENT POUR TOI, CHAMPION ?

TU VOTERAS POUR QUI TU VOUDRAS, MAIS CE QUE JE VEUX, C'EST QUE TU M'AIDES À GAGNER !

J'AI BESOIN D'UN HOMME COMME TOI. UNE CAMPAGNE ÉLECTORALE N'EST PAS QU'UNE PARTIE DE PLAISIR. VOUS POURRIEZ, TOI ET TES RELATIONS, DISCRÈTEMENT RÉGLER CERTAINS PROBLÈMES S'ILS VENAIENT À SE POSER.

TU SAIS, JE VIENS D'OUVRIR CE CABINET, CHEZ MOI, EN VIRGINIE... MES QUELQUES PROCÈS TRÈS MÉDIATISÉS M'ONT BIEN LANCÉ...

TU NE VAS PAS PASSER TA CARRIÈRE D'AVOCAT À DÉFENDRE DES TYPES COMME CE CANNIBALE EN ALABAMA OU ENCORE CET ÉTRANGLEUR DE CHICAGO! CES DÉVIANTS TE FASCINENT, OU QUOI?

LES NOIRS ONT BIEN DROIT À UN AVOCAT, POURQUOI PAS LES TUEURS EN SÉRIE?

POUR TON FRÈRE, J'ÉTAIS L'HOMME QUI LUI OUVRIRAIT UN JOUR LES PORTES DU SUD PROFOND, CE DIXIELAND CONFÉDÉRÉ, TERRE DU KLAN HOSTILE AUX DÉMOCRATES.

DE MON CÔTÉ, JE TENAIS LA MARIONNETTE QUI ALLAIT FAIRE REGRETTER AUX RÉPUBLICAINS DE M'AVOIR RENIÉ POUR MES IDÉES SOI-DISANT TROP EXTRÊMES...

UNE FOIS DE PLUS, NOUS ÉTIONS FAITS POUR NOUS ENTENDRE.

JE SUIS DEVENU L'HOMME DE L'OMBRE DE WILLIAM SHERIDAN.

ALLONS, WALLY, NE FAIS PAS L'ENFANT...
TU SAIS PARFAITEMENT DE QUOI SONT FAITES LES ARRIÈRE-CUISINES DES CAMPAGNES ÉLECTORALES.

JE VEUX DES BARRAGES ROUTIERS
SUR LES 4 AXES PRINCIPAUX DE
WASHINGTON DÈS LUNDI MATIN
ET TU CASSERAS CETTE GRÈVE
DÈS QU'ON TE LE DEMANDERA !

NO
WAY !

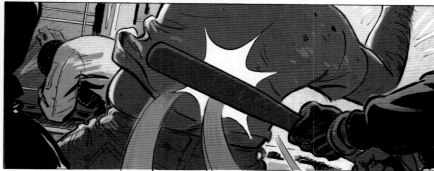

LAISSEZ-LE !
ON A BESOIN
DE LUI
VIVANT !

LE SYNDICAT DES CAMION-
NEURS A TOUJOURS ÉTÉ
SENSIBLE AUX INTÉRÊTS QUE
JE REPRÉSENTE. FAIS CE
QU'ON TE DIT ET TU N'AURAS
PAS À LE REGRETTER.

MARCHÉ
CONCLU ?

CHANTAGE, PRESSION, COERCITION, EXTORSION, POT-DE-VIN, TRAHISON, J'AI EMBRASSÉ ET DIGÉRÉ TOUTES LES FAIBLESSES ET PERVERSIONS HUMAINES POUR LES TRANSFORMER UNE À UNE EN AVANTAGES POLITIQUES!!!

J'AI DONNÉ DES COUPS ET J'EN AI REÇU ...

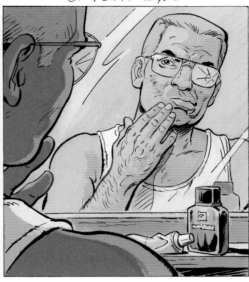

SANS JAMAIS ME PLAINDRE À PERSONNE.

LA POLITIQUE EST UNE AFFAIRE D'HOMMES SOLITAIRES ...

..QUI SOIGNENT LEURS PLAIES À L'ÉCART DU MONDE !!!

ET POUR RÉPONDRE À TA QUESTION, JE N'AI FAIT **QUE** DES CHOSES ILLÉGALES POUR TON FRÈRE.

EN TANT QU'AVOCAT, J'AI CONTRIBUÉ À ARRONDIR DES ANGLES DEVENUS TROP TRANCHANTS À FORCE DE JOUER AVEC LES LIMITES DU FINANCEMENT DES CAMPAGNES ÉLECTORALES.

J'AI DÉFENDU GRATUITEMENT DES VOYOUS POUR LES TRANSFORMER EN SOLDATS INFÉODÉS À TON FRÈRE...

J'AI NÉGOCIÉ EN SECRET DES ACCORDS AVEC DES PARTENAIRES AVEC QUI LE CANDIDAT SHERIDAN NE POUVAIT PAS OFFICIELLEMENT S'AFFICHER...

ET NOUS AVONS GAGNÉ.

EN QUELQUES MOIS, J'ÉTAIS DEVENU UN BEAU SALOPARD AU SERVICE D'UNE CAUSE QUI N'ÉTAIT MÊME PAS LA MIENNE !

MAIS TON FRÈRE ÉTAIT DÉPUTÉ, DIRECTION L'AILE SUD DU CAPITOLE ! SON ASCENSION ÉTAIT DÉSORMAIS INEXORABLE ...

... ET C'EST TOUT CE QUI M'IMPORTAIT.

L'ENTOURAGE DU PRÉSIDENT SHERIDAN A CONFIRMÉ L'ORGANISATION D'UNE GRANDE TOURNÉE DANS LES ÉTATS DU SUD D'ICI QUELQUES MOIS...

...TOUT SEMBLE INDIQUER SA VOLONTÉ D'ACCOMPLIR UN SECOND MANDAT.

LA FIN DES ANNÉES 60 !

JE ME SOUVIENS DE CETTE ÉPOQUE, J'ÉTAIS ÉTUDIANT, TOUT SEMBLAIT ALLER VITE ET DANS LE BON SENS, MÊME LA GUERRE AU VIÊTNAM JOUAIT EN NOTRE FAVEUR.

WILLIAM AVAIT À PEINE TERMINÉ DE FAIRE REPEINDRE SON BUREAU À LA CHAMBRE DES REPRÉSENTANTS, QU'À TABLE, AVEC PAPA, IL PARLAIT DÉJÀ DE GAGNER LE SÉNAT !

TON FRÈRE AVAIT L'AMBITION, L'INTELLIGENCE MAIS AUSSI DE LA PATIENCE ET BEAUCOUP DE SANG-FROID ! LE PARTI DÉMOCRATE S'OFFRAIT À LUI ! LES OBSERVATEURS LE VOYAIENT DÉJÀ PRÉSIDENT ! MAIS C'ÉTAIT COMPTER SANS LA GRANDE FAIBLESSE DES SHERIDAN...

...LES FEMMES !

DURANT LES 9 ANNÉES QUI LUI ONT ÉTÉ NÉCESSAIRES POUR DEVENIR SÉNATEUR DU DELAWARE, IL Y A EU TOUTES CES FILLES DE LA JET-SET, CES AVENTURES D'UN SOIR, VOIRE DE 15 MINUTES, FACILES À CONTRÔLER ET À OUBLIER... IL Y A EU AUSSI DES LIAISONS PLUS LONGUES, COMPLIQUÉES, ET QUI PARFOIS SE SONT TERMINÉES EN DRAME.

DES HISTOIRES SORDIDES OÙ L'ON FINISSAIT TOUJOURS PAR FAIRE APPEL À MES TALENTS ... COMME AVEC CETTE FEMME MÉDECIN ... TU T'EN SOUVIENS PEUT-ÊTRE...

IL L'A RENCONTRÉE LE JOUR DES 20 ANS DE JANET, TA FUTURE FEMME.

HAPPY BIRTH

J'AI SU IMMÉDIATEMENT QU'IL EN TOMBERAIT AMOUREUX.

QUI EST CETTE FILLE ?

MARTHA SHOEBRIDGE, MÉDECIN, MILITANTE PRO-AVORTEMENT.

TU TE RENDS COMPTE, TON FRÈRE ET UNE OBSTÉTRICIENNE PRO-AVORTEMENT ! SI LES RÉPUBLICAINS L'APPRENAIENT, C'EN ÉTAIT FINI DE SA CARRIÈRE !

JE ME SOUVIENS D'ELLE, J'AVOUE MÊME AVOIR FAIT UN PEU L'ENTREMETTEUR UN SOIR SUR LE YACHT DES FITZSIMMONS ! BONNE DANSEUSE ; ELLE A SOMBRÉ DANS L'ALCOOL, JE CROIS.

LEUR LIAISON A DURÉ, ET IL A MÊME ENVISAGÉ DE L'ÉPOUSER !

IL L'AIMAIT, C'ÉTAIT CERTAIN !

J'AI CORROMPU DES MILITANTS POUR QU'ILS POUSSENT MARTHA À DEVENIR PRÉSIDENTE DU COMITÉ D'AIDE MÉDICALE AUX INDIGENTS, PUIS J'AI RÉVÉLÉ L'INFORMATION À WILLIAM EN LUI EXPLIQUANT QUE LA PRESSE, QUI VENAIT DE DÉCOUVRIR QU'ELLE MILITAIT AUSSI POUR L'AVORTEMENT, N'ALLAIT PAS TARDER À SAVOIR QU'ELLE PASSAIT SES SOIRÉES ET SES WEEK-ENDS À DISCUTER AVEC LUI !

ALORS IL A FALLU AGIR.

ADIEU MARTHA, LA FAISEUSE D'ANGES, BONJOUR CORDULA WEST, FILLE DE LA PLUS GROSSE FORTUNE MINIÈRE DE VIRGINIE !

À CETTE ÉPOQUE, TA CHARMANTE BELLE-SŒUR SAVAIT ÉCOUTER MES CONSEILS ; AU MOMENT OPPORTUN, ET À MON SIGNAL, ELLE L'A REMIS DANS SON LIT.

À SON BRAS, WILLIAM POUVAIT SEREINEMENT S'EN ALLER GAGNER CES FICHUES SÉNATORIALES.

À PEINE AVAIT-IL ENDOSSÉ LE COSTUME DE SÉNATEUR DU DELAWARE QUE TON FRÈRE REPRENAIT SES MAUVAISES HABITUDES, UNE FILLE PAR-CI, UNE AUTRE PAR-LÀ, PARFOIS DEUX DIFFÉRENTES DANS LA MÊME JOURNÉE ...

MAIS LA NOUVELLE CATASTROPHE EST ARRIVÉE DEUX ANS APRÈS SON ÉLECTION, ELLE SE NOMMAIT ALYSON ... MILITANTE DÉMOCRATE ...

CELLE-LÀ, COMME UNE RÉPONSE DU SEIGNEUR À SON AVENTURE AVEC L'AVORTEUSE, IL L'A MISE ENCEINTE ET NE L'A APPRIS QUE 6 MOIS PLUS TARD !

?

?

SALETÉ !

TU AS L'AIR D'AVOIR DES REMORDS AU SUJET DE CETTE HISTOIRE...

... CALVIN, QU'EST-CE QU'IL S'EST PASSÉ ?

LA FILLE NE POUVAIT PLUS LÉGALE-MENT AVORTER... AVANT DE FAIRE APPEL À DES ITALIENS MAFIEUX, DES AMIS DE VOTRE PÈRE, POUR RÉGLER LE PRO-BLÈME, IL M'A CONSUL-TÉ, COMME TOUJOURS.

JE LUI AI DIT QUE LES MACARONIS LE FERAIENT CHANTER TÔT OU TARD S'IL LEUR DEMANDAIT UN TEL SERVICE... IL VALAIT MIEUX QU'ON S'EN OCCUPE TOUS LES DEUX.

ALORS J'AI IMAGINÉ UN PLAN DIABOLIQUE POUR NOUS DÉBARRASSER DE LA FILLE, DU BÉBÉ ET EN PRIME, FAIRE PORTER LE CHAPEAU À MARTHA, L'OBSTÉTRICIENNE AVORTEUSE.

JE LUI AI FOURNI DU L.S.D. QU'IL N'AVAIT PLUS QU'À FAIRE AVALER À ALYSON, MÉLANGÉ À DE L'ASPIRINE POUR PROVOQUER UNE FAUSSE COUCHE.

NOUS AVONS PRIS LA VIE D'UN ENFANT INNOCENT, WALLY ...

34

POUR DEVENIR PRÉSIDENT, IL FALLAIT D'ABORD QUE WILLIAM REMPORTE LES PRIMAIRES DÉMOCRATES...

MAIS CETTE HISTOIRE DE MÈRE MORTE AVEC SON BÉBÉ LE HANTAIT...

ELLE AVAIT ÉGALEMENT MENÉ LA BELLE DOCTEUR MARTHA À LA DÉCHÉANCE.

ALORS IL A ÉCHOUÉ.

TON FRÈRE A PERDU CES PRIMAIRES CONTRE DUKAKIS PARCE QU'AU FOND, IL N'ÉTAIT PAS TOTALEMENT DÉTERMINÉ À LES REMPORTER !... EN POLITIQUE, CETTE FAIBLESSE NE PARDONNE PAS.

MÊME S'IL N'A JAMAIS VOULU L'ADMETTRE.

CE NE SONT QUE DES RÉSULTATS PARTIELS !...

ATTENDONS LA CALIFORNIE !

TES RÉSULTATS SONT PARTIELS, MAIS MA DÉFAITE EST **TOTALE !** ABRUTI !!!

JE VAIS TE ...

WILLIAM, ARRÊTE ! **CALME-TOI !**

C'EST PERDU, INUTILE DE SE MENTIR, MAIS CE N'EST QUE PARTIE REMISE, JE FERAI TOUT POUR TOI, TU LE SAIS.

TU ES MON AMI, CALVIN.

ET ?

TU NE DIS PLUS RIEN ...

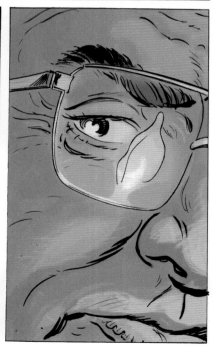

LES QUATRE ANNÉES QUI ONT SUIVI CETTE DÉFAITE AUX PRIMAIRES ONT ÉTÉ CELLES DE SA RECONSTRUCTION, PUIS DE SON INEXORABLE CONQUÊTE.

D'ABORD CE FUT LA COURSE À L'INVESTITURE DÉMOCRATE, PUIS LA CAMPAGNE PRÉSIDENTIELLE.

LE VIEUX SUD, COMME TOUJOURS, ALLAIT ÊTRE DÉCISIF.

J'Y AVAIS GARDÉ CERTAINES RELATIONS QUI ALLAIENT PORTER LEURS FRUITS.

DEPUIS TRUMAN, ON SAVAIT QUE LE PARTI DÉMOCRATE ENTRETENAIT DES LIENS AMBIGUS AVEC LE KLAN ...,

MOI, J'Y COMPTE QUELQUES BONS AMIS.

DES HOMMES QU'IL A FALLU CONVAINCRE D'AIDER TON FRÈRE À GAGNER.

DES PATRIOTES COMME DWIGHT S. RIGBY...,

AU FUTUR GRAND DRAGON DU COLORADO !

ALORS, CALVIN, PARLE-MOI DE TON POULAIN! QU'EST-CE QUE TU ATTENDS DE MOI ?

TU ES UN HOMME INFLUENT, UN PATRON PUISSANT... ON DIT MÊME QUE TU VAS RACHETER LE JOURNAL DE GREENFALLS.

POUR MON CRÉTIN DE FILS QUI VEUT DEVENIR JOURNALISTE, C'EST VRAI !

NOUS SAVONS QUE TU AURAS BESOIN D'UN PETIT COUP DE POUCE POUR TRANSFORMER TON ROYAUME EN EMPIRE DANS LES ANNÉES À VENIR.

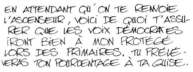

EN ATTENDANT QU'ON TE RENVOIE L'ASCENSEUR, VOICI DE QUOI T'ASSURER QUE LES VOIX DÉMOCRATES IRONT BIEN À MON PROTÉGÉ LORS DES PRIMAIRES. TU PRÉLÈVERAS TON POURCENTAGE À TA GUISE.

QU'EST-CE QUE TU FRICOTES AVEC CE SHERIDAN, CALVIN, TU AVAIS PLUS D'AVENIR DANS NOTRE BON VIEUX SUD.

KEEP AMERICA AMERICAN !!!

AVEC LUI, LE SYSTÈME FÉDÉRAL S'ÉCROULERA PLUS VITE, C'EST NOTRE MEILLEURE CHANCE DE RÉTABLIR LES VALEURS SÉGRÉGATIONNISTES AVANT LA FIN DU SIÈCLE !

PENDANT DEUX ANS, J'AI PACTISÉ AVEC DES ALLIÉS DE L'OMBRE, OPÉRÉ D'IMPROBABLES ALLIANCES ET DES RAPPROCHEMENTS QUASI CONTRE NATURE...

J'AI OUVERT À TON FRÈRE TOUTES LES TABLES DE MA FAMILLE, JE ME SUIS ASSURÉ QUE TOUS LES DIXIECRATS * LE SOUTIENDRAIENT.

TES AMIS HELLS ANGELS, PASSE ENCORE, CALVIN, MAIS FRANCHEMENT, COMMENT PEUX-TU FRÉQUENTER LE KLAN ?

PARCE QUE C'EST DANS MA NATURE !

MALGRÉ MON ÉDUCATION, MES DIPLÔMES, MON CABINET D'AVOCAT, LE POUVOIR ET L'ARGENT QU'OFFRENT LA CÔTE EST, MA PLACE EST DANS CETTE AMÉRIQUE PROFONDE QUI DÉFEND LE POUVOIR DE L'HOMME BLANC PROTESTANT. JE SUIS DE LINCOLN, NEBRASKA.

ET MON FRÈRE SAIT TOUT ÇA ?

TON FRÈRE M'A ORDONNÉ DE PASSER DISCRÈTEMENT TOUS CES PACTES, IL NE S'EST JAMAIS ENGAGÉ PERSONNELLEMENT, BIEN ENTENDU, MAIS TU NE CROIS TOUT DE MÊME PAS QUE J'AI FINANCÉ TOUS CES PATRIOTES AVEC MES ÉCONOMIES ?

TON PÈRE M'A FOURNI DES FONDS, WALLY, IL A TOUJOURS SOUTENU LA CARRIÈRE DE TON FRÈRE, TANDIS QU'IL TE LAISSAIT CONDUIRE LA TIENNE AVEC UNE CERTAINE INDIFFÉRENCE.

POUR ARRANGER LES AFFAIRES DE TON PÈRE, J'AI DÛ FAIRE ACTE D'ALLÉGEANCE À L'ÉGARD DE CETTE MAFIA MACARONI CATHOLIQUE, LA FAMILLE GIORDINO ! QU'ILS BRÛLENT TOUS EN ENFER !

* ÉLUS DÉMOCRATES MAIS ULTRACONSERVATEURS DU SUD.

NOUS AVONS REMPORTÉ LES PRIMAIRES HAUT LA MAIN ET, GRÂCE AU CONTEXTE POLITIQUE INTERNATIONAL, LA PRÉSIDENTIELLE NE FUT QU'UNE FORMALITÉ. JE FUS MÊME DÉSIGNÉ POUR SUPERVISER LA CAMPAGNE POUR LA VICE-PRÉSIDENCE DE CE BALOURD DE GALBRAIN DONT J'ÉTAIS LE CONSEILLER ÉCONOMIQUE.

RAPPELLE-TOI, TOUS CES HIPPIES DÉGÉNÉRÉS QUI APPELAIENT À VOTER POUR NOUS, C'ÉTAIT MAGNIFIQUE. MON TRIOMPHE ÉTAIT TOTAL! JE PENSAIS TOUT MAÎTRISER... LE DÉPARTEMENT D'ÉTAT M'ÉTAIT QUASIMENT RÉSERVÉ.

MAIS J'AI COMPRIS QUI ÉTAIT LE VRAI MANIPULATEUR DE L'HISTOIRE LE JOUR DE LA VICTOIRE DE TON FRÈRE AUX ÉLECTIONS PRÉSIDENTIELLES, IL Y A DEUX ANS.

LE MARDI QUI SUIT LE PREMIER LUNDI DE NOVEMBRE... "ÉLECTION DAY".

NOUS FÊTIONS LA VICTOIRE DANS LE Q.G. DE CAMPAGNE DE NEW YORK. DEPUIS L'ANNONCE DES RÉSULTATS, J'AVAIS TROUVÉ WILLIAM DISTANT ENVERS MOI...

IL ÉVITAIT MÊME DE CROISER MON REGARD...

QUAND SOUDAIN...

CALVIN...

TU ME SUIS, IL FAUT QU'ON PARLE!

WILLIAM, NOUS Y SOMMES !

TU AS FAIT UN EXCELLENT TRAVAIL AUPRÈS DE GALBRAIN. JE VEUX QUE TU RESTES AVEC LUI, POUR LE CONSEILLER, BIEN ENTENDU, MAIS SURTOUT POUR LE SURVEILLER.

JE NE TE CACHE PAS QUE JE M'ATTENDAIS À QUELQUE CHOSE DE PLUS ENGAGÉ À TES CÔTÉS... LA JUSTICE, PEUT-ÊTRE...

TU ES MON PLUS FIDÈLE LIEUTENANT, CALVIN, MAIS TES RELATIONS AMBIGUËS AVEC TOUS CES NAZILLONS SÉCESSIONNISTES COMMENCENT À FAIRE JASER. T'AVOIR AVEC MOI SERAIT DONNER UN BÂTON AUX JOURNALISTES POUR ME FAIRE BATTRE.

POUR LA JUSTICE, J'AI PLUTÔT PENSÉ À SMITH.

SMITH? MAIS IL... ENFIN, IL EST HOMOSEXUEL !

QU'EST-CE QUI TE GÊNE ? JE NE TE DEMANDE PAS DE PRENDRE TES DOUCHES AVEC LUI !

BIEN, MONSIEUR LE PRÉSIDENT.

CE FUT LA DERNIÈRE FOIS QUE JE LE RENCONTRAI EN TÊTE À TÊTE ...

ON ARRIVE.

41

CAFÉ ?

JE VEUX BIEN ...

QUE DOIS-TU ME MONTRER D'IMPORTANT ?

J'AI SURTOUT UNE PROPOSITION À TE FAIRE, MAIS EFFECTIVEMENT, AVANT TOUT, TU DOIS VOIR UN DOCUMENT ...

...CETTE VIDÉO.

C'EST PARTI !

JULIA ...

WIL ...

FILMÉS ENSEMBLE, MON DIEU ...

C'EST LE LOFT DE JULIA À LOS ANGELES !

CLIC

DANS LES JOURNAUX À SCANDALE DE LA CÔTE OUEST, ON APPELLE ÇA UNE SEXTAPE ...

DANS LE JARGON DES SERVICES SECRETS, ÇA SE TRADUIT PAR : « CHANTAGE ORGANISÉ ».

PAR QUI ?

TA PETITE AMIE FAISAIT CHANTER LE PRÉSIDENT, WALLY... ELLE A ORGANISÉ LE TOURNAGE DE CE FILM AVEC SON AMANT TU SAIS, CE JUNKIE QU'ELLE VENAIT SOI-DISANT DE QUITTER ET QUI A ÉTÉ RETROUVÉ MORT HIER D'UNE OVERDOSE À NEW YORK.

JE LE SAIS PARCE QUE MES HOMMES L'ONT LIQUIDÉ APRÈS LUI AVOIR FAIT AVOUER OÙ IL CACHAIT CE MAUDIT FILM ET LES COPIES VHS ...

MAIS ENFIN, POURQUOI FAISAIT-ELLE CHANTER MON FRÈRE ?

WALLY !... JE T'AI MENTI EN TE DISANT QUE JE N'AVAIS PLUS PARLÉ AVEC TON FRÈRE DEPUIS SON ÉLECTION...

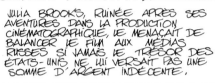

ELLE ÉTAIT DROGUÉE ET AUX ABOIS ! C'EST PARFOIS SUFFISANT POUR COMMETTRE L'IRRÉPARABLE !

IL EST VENU ME TROUVER IL Y A DEUX SEMAINES.

JULIA BROOKS, RUINÉE APRÈS SES AVENTURES DANS LA PRODUCTION CINÉMATOGRAPHIQUE, LE MENAÇAIT DE BALANCER LE FILM AUX MÉDIAS RUSSES SI JAMAIS LE TRÉSOR DES ÉTATS-UNIS NE LUI VERSAIT PAS UNE SOMME D'ARGENT INDÉCENTE.

WILLIAM M'A DEMANDÉ DE RÉCUPÉRER LE FILM ET DE FAIRE LE MÉNAGE. TOUT LE MÉNAGE... COMME AU BON VIEUX TEMPS...

JULIA !... J'IGNORAIS QU'IL LA CONNAISSAIT, ELLE ÉTAIT À MOI !

TON FRÈRE A TOUJOURS TOUT EU AVANT TOI, WALLY, ET QUAND CE FUT L'INVERSE, IL TE L'A TOUJOURS VOLÉ NON ?

CETTE NUIT... C'EST...

...C'EST TOI QUI AS TUÉ JULIA...

NE ME FAIS PAS DIRE CE QUE JE N'AI PAS DIT... JE SUIS LÀ POUR TON BIEN, WALLY.

44

MAIS POUR CETTE SEXTAPE... IL TE SOUPÇONNE D'AVOIR TOUT ORGANISÉ AVEC JULIA POUR LE PIÉGER.

QUOI ? C'EST RIDICULE !

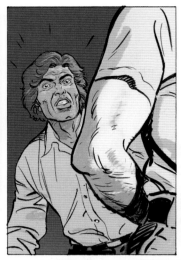

TU AS TUÉ JULIA !...

ET MAINTENANT C'EST MON TOUR, N'EST-CE PAS ?!!

NE FAIS PAS L'ENFANT, WALLY !

?

CE TYPE ! JE L'AI VU CETTE NUIT... À LA POMPE À ESSENCE !

NORMAL, IL NOUS ESCORTAIT DISCRÈTEMENT...

45

IL PREND LE SENTIER DES PENDUS !

IL VA SE PERDRE !

JE VAIS LE CHERCHER, SEUL !

KLAC

TU VAS Y LAISSER TA PAIRE DE WESTON, WALLY !

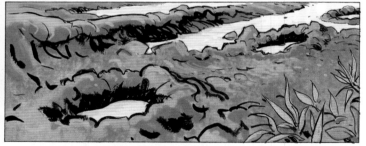

46

47

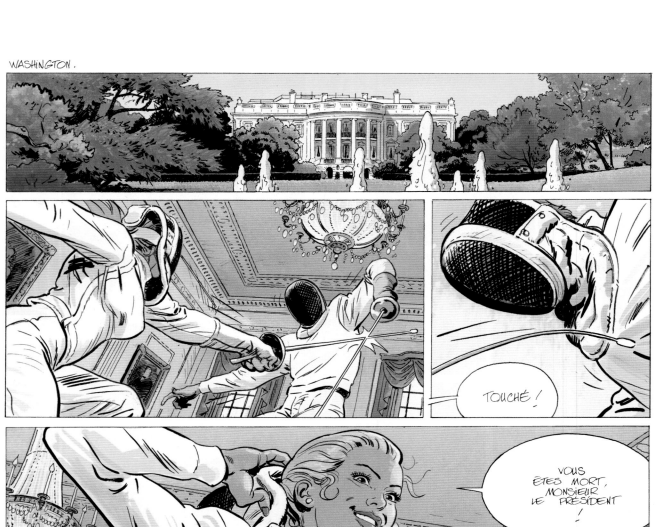

TOUCHÉ !

VOUS ÊTES MORT, MONSIEUR LE PRÉSIDENT !

IL FUT UN TEMPS OÙ MA PARADE ET MON CONTRE AURAIENT EU RAISON DE TOI !... JE SUIS ÉPUISÉ, ON ARRÊTE POUR AUJOURD'HUI, RACHEL.

SPADASSIN DE MON CŒUR !

TU AURAIS DÛ M'ÉCOUTER ET DORMIR UN PEU CETTE NUIT...

À LA SEMAINE PROCHAINE, MONSIEUR LE PRÉSIDENT, NOUS REVERRONS QUELQUES BOTTES POUR AMÉLIORER VOTRE DÉFENSE.

J'EMPRUNTE UNE DE VOS SALLES DE BAIN !

QUE VOULEZ-VOUS ?

VOTRE COMMUNIQUÉ AU SUJET DU DÉCÈS DE LA COMÉDIENNE JULIA BROOKS, MONSIEUR LE PRÉSIDENT.

GN... GN... GN... GN... GN... « JULIA BROOKS VIVRA ÉTERNELLEMENT »... TRÈS BIEN, ÇA !

PAR CONTRE, VOUS RETIREZ TOUT CE QUI ÉVOQUE SA VIE PRIVÉE, JE PARLE AU NOM DE L'AMÉRIQUE, AUCUNE INTIMITÉ NE DOIT TRANSPARAÎTRE.

BIEN, MONSIEUR LE PRÉSIDENT.

DES NOUVELLES DE MON FRÈRE ?

AUCUNE DEPUIS L'ANNONCE DU DÉCÈS DE MISS BROOKS, MONSIEUR LE PRÉSIDENT.

SON ASSISTANT ET SON ÉPOUSE SAVENT SIMPLEMENT QU'IL EST EN WEEK-END AVEC DES AMIS D'UNIVERSITÉ POUR UNE PARTIE DE PÊCHE OU DE CHASSE...

...IL EST EN TOUT CAS INJOIGNABLE.

SACRÉ WALLY, TOUJOURS DANS NOS PATTES QUAND IL DEVRAIT SE FAIRE TOUT PETIT, MAIS JAMAIS LÀ QUAND IL LE FAUT !

C'EST POUR ÇA QU'IL NE RÉUSSIRA JAMAIS EN POLITIQUE !

50

NE... NE ME TUE PAS !

JE N'AI JAMAIS EU L'INTENTION DE TE TUER, WALLY... QUOI QUE J'AIE PU PROMETTRE AU PRÉSIDENT SHERIDAN.

J'APPARTIENS À UN GROUPE DE HAUTS RESPONSABLES QUI ESTIME QUE S'IL FAUT ÉLIMINER UN MEMBRE DE TA FAMILLE DEVENU UN DANGER POUR L'AMÉRIQUE, C'EST TON FRÈRE.

NOUS ALLONS RETOURNER CHEZ MOI, TU PRENDRAS UNE DOUCHE ET BILLY BOY NOUS PRÉPARERA UN T-BONE STEAK DONT IL A LE SECRET, PUIS TU ÉCOUTERAS MA PROPOSITION.

CE SALAUD A FAIT TUER LA PLUS BELLE FEMME D'AMÉRIQUE... JE LE HAIS...

JE LE HAIS DEPUIS TOUJOURS...

LE CORPS SANS VIE DE JULIA BROOKS A ÉTÉ DÉCOUVERT CET APRÈS-MIDI DANS SA MAISON DE WASHINGTON D.C.

LES ENQUÊTEURS ÉVOQUENT UN SUICIDE SUITE À LA MORT DE SON AMI, LE METTEUR EN SCÈNE MIKE POWELL...

ÉTEINS ÇA, CALVIN, S'IL TE PLAÎT.

BIEN !

LA CONJURATION DES XX EST AU COMPLET !

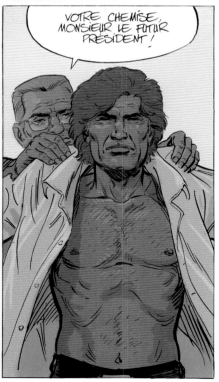

VOTRE CHEMISE, MONSIEUR LE FUTUR PRÉSIDENT !

NETTOYAGE TERMINÉ, M. WAX !...

...M. SHERIDAN N'EST JAMAIS ENTRÉ DANS LA VILLA DE MISS BROOKS.

BEAU TRAVAIL, PAUL.

M. SHERIDAN EST-IL ENCORE PARMI NOUS ?

OUI, IL SE REPOSE À CÔTÉ.

AVEZ-VOUS SU LE CONVAINCRE ?

NOUS AVONS NOTRE NUMÉRO I, PAUL !

UN RÉGIME AUTORITAIRE DIRIGERA BIENTÔT CE PAYS D'UNE MAIN DE FER !

MESSIEURS ...JE PROPOSE DE NOUS OFFRIR UNE BONNE PARTIE DE CHASSE DEMAIN MATIN !

ACCIDENT DE TIR!

RRGH RRRGLRHL

KLAC

PFiiuu

iuuiiuu

CALVIN!
...

POURQUOI?

55

À PART MOI, NUL NE CONNAÎTRA L'IDENTITÉ DU NUMÉRO I.

IL FAUT SE DÉBARRASSER DES CORPS. J'AI LES OUTILS AU PAVILLON DE CHASSE...

AU TRAVAIL, WALLY !

CALVIN !... SI TU REVOIS MON FRÈRE !...

...QUE LUI DIRAS-TU ?

QUE NUL N'ÉCHAPPE À SON DESTIN.

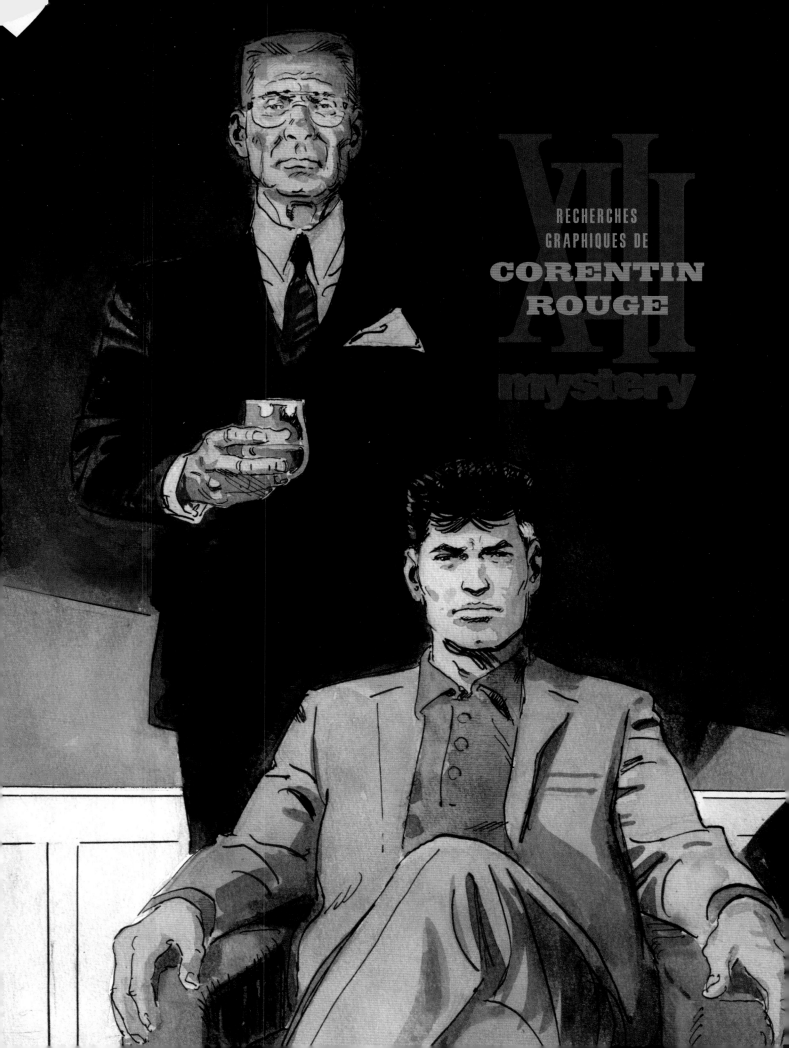

RECHERCHES
GRAPHIQUES DE
CORENTIN
ROUGE

mystery

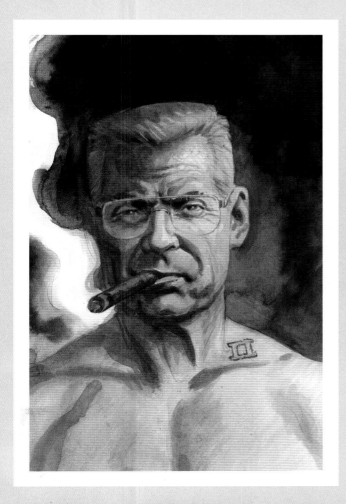